WHITE TIGER QIGONG™



五元氣功

# 5 Element Qigong

## 5 Ancient Qigong Exercises for Ultimate Health and Longevity Fascia and Chinese Medicine in Qigong

BY Tevia Feng

**ISBN** 9781940085098



www.whitetigerqigong.com

五元氣功

# Foreword

*"When I let go of who I am, I become what I might be."*

TAO TE CHING BY LAO TZU

If you were to ask me to describe the author of this book in one sentence, I would say:

"Master Tevia Feng is a master of his craft, - a powerhouse; he lives and breathes Qigong, fully practicing what he preaches, and inspires people from all walks of life, nations and ages to journey into energy cultivation and to make a commitment to it."

Bringing his original blend of traditional Qigong practices, combined with modern sports science and fascia research to the printed word, Tevia provides here a holistic approach to learning about Five Element Qigong. He has over three decades of experience and intensive training to draw upon, runs his successful White Tiger Qigong school, and has developed numerous printed and audio-visual materials in this field.

Tevia wants Qigong to be an approachable modality, so this book is broken down into easily accessible sections: taking you on a journey to the mountains of China, sharing Qigong principles, guiding you through the practices with clear pictures and instructions, and helping you to understand the short and long-term results of making Five Element Qigong a regular part of your life.

He stresses the importance of developing sensitivity to one's inner landscape during practice, so that the profound effects this Qigong has at both the superficial and deeper levels of the body, mind and spirit can be more fully grasped. We get out of Qigong what we are willing to put in, and if we practice consistently, we can effect long-lasting changes to our entire fascia, nervous system and posture – and, of course, our energy flow!

As one of Master Tevia's students, I hope that this book will either be used as a useful adjunct to having already trained with him, or inspire you to seek out one of his schools one day.

The written word can provide an insightful learning platform, and this book is no exception. Still, I hope for your benefit that you will one day get to put into practice with Tevia what you have learnt here. Nothing beats the experience of training with the Master in the flesh!

**SARAH DIVINE**

*White Tiger Qigong Instructor and Student*

treated me to a noodle stand at the roadside. In the next few days, they upgraded my accommodation a couple of times, each place better than the previous. I started to realize that the little old man in the ragged clothing commanded the monk. I thought that he was likely the boss and I was intrigued. He was originally very unassuming and had me believe that he was merely along for the ride. Every day he said, *"I don't know that much, but..."* and then he would teach me about the *"I-Ching"*. Eventually he invited me to stay at his home, which I was surprised to find was a palace! The tea table alone was worth 100,000 USD. He was drinking tea that cost tens of thousands of dollars. He said to me, *"When you meet a real Taoist master, you will not know who he is, as he hides his real powers."*

The little old man in the rags and the taped Northface jacket turned out to be the Abbot of Tien Ji Tao sect, a secret sect of Taoism. His master fled during the communist revolution and was a Taoist nun who passed the lineage down to him. *"How did you get so much money?"* I asked. *"Money is a game to me."* he replied. *"I dress in rags. I used the "I-Ching" to do business like a game. When you really understand "I-Ching", you can play everything like a fiddle."*

I ended up living with him in this spectacular palace and he would teach me all day. He never charged me a dime, and gave me this amazing knowledge. I became the only foreigner to ever study with this sect. As I met the few other disciples, I realized that all were very carefully chosen.

There are many Qigong teachers who teach as a hobby. I have dedicated my life to this path, and I've been lucky to travel the world and meet many different teachers, who have become the source of all this wisdom. Speaking Mandarin also helped as it opened a world most foreigners never get to experience. I have been given inside information, and I care about putting it together in a way that the Western mind can understand.

**Tevia Feng**

*Master Instructor, Creator & Founder of White Tiger Qigong™*

五元氣功

# Contents

# How to Read This Book

STORIES, THEORY AND PRACTICE

This book was written in a formula that will allow you to take in the information in multiple ways, through:

- Clear instructions for your physical practice.
- The theories behind these practices and the connection to Western thinking about physiology and the mind.
- Connections to modern fascia research, sports science and how to apply this learning to your own situation.
- Connections to Chinese medicine theory

Each animal chapter is structured as a sequence of:

- Physical Forms and Movement
- Qigong Theory and Background

### Physical Forms and Movement

While a book cannot teach you the exact way to move with the physical forms of Qigong, it is an excellent companion to working with a qualified Qigong teacher. In order to get the greatest value from this book, we recommend that you work directly with a White Tiger Qigong teacher as you read through each of the animals in order to learn the physical form. We have created an online course that is the perfect companion to this book so you can actually see what the movements are like. You can also try it on your own using videos of Qigong practitioners out there on YouTube for free, but we must point out that many Qigong masters intentionally leave out important elements of the form when filmed, in order to preserve the secret teachings for in-person transmission.

## Qigong Theory and Background

Qigong Theory is comprised of several major components. In this section, we will explore each one. Each element is part of a holistic view of the world popularized in Chinese Medicine. The 5 elements of Chinese Medicine are Water, Earth, Fire, Wood, and Metal. Each element plays an important role in using this Qigong for mental, physical, and emotional clarity and well-being.

五元氣功

# About this *Qigong*

## How Is This 5 Element Qigong Different?

The 5 Element Qigong system covered in this book includes five powerful forms, named after five powerful animals. Each form is associated with an element, a color, an organ, an emotion, a season, a direction and more.

| | Dragon | Tiger | Leopard | Snake | Crane |
|---|---|---|---|---|---|
| Element | Water | Metal | Wood | Earth | Fire |
| Color | Blue/ Black | White | Green | Yellow | Red |
| Zang | Kidney | Lung | Liver | Spleen | Heart |
| Fu Organ | Bladder | Large Intestine | Gallbladder | Stomach | Small Intestine/ Triple Burner |
| Emotion | Fear | Grief | Anger | Anxiety | Joy |
| Direction | North | West | East | Center | South |
| Season | Winter | Fall | Spring | Late Summer | Summer |

This dynamic form combines deep rhythmic movements of five different animals, Qigong meditation, deep Qigong breathing techniques and a strong, focused spirit. Each animal form works to heal and bring into balance the internal organs and the meridians of the body. These animal forms each represent a different element of the 5 Elements of Chinese Medicine, which are each associated with a different internal organ and related meridian.

This Qigong works by squeezing out toxins and emotions out of the organs like a sponge, then dynamically stretching the body to open the area up leaving you feeling peaceful, relaxed and focused.

五元氣功

# Key Principles *of* 5 Element Qigong

## The 3 Adjustments of 5 Element Qigong

### Form

For each animal movement, proper alignment stance-work is crucial in order to correctly engage the rest of the body, and to open the hips and meridians properly. This also sets the stage for the core to be actively engaged, which helps open the rest of the body.

**Expansion/Retraction, Contraction and Relaxation:**
Each animal movement has an expansion or retraction phase as well as a contraction phase. Finally, you have the relaxation phase which is in the Zhan Zhuang posture following the completion of each animal. This follows in alignment with the Yin/Yang principle. If you leave out one of these phases, it is not in accordance with the principles of Yin and Yang and is therefore incorrect.

It is important to reach to your maximum point in each movement without straining. If you notice your body starts to shake during the movement, you may be straining too hard in your efforts to reach your maximum. There is a fine balance point between reaching your maximum and putting in too much effort. The key words are 'gentle' and 'gradual'.

**Vision Guides the Movement:**
Your vision should either be at your hand or at a point in front of you that you are reaching for. For example, in Dragon, if you want to reach a little further, look at a point a little further than where your hand is, trying to reach for that area. If this is uncomfortable, just look at the palm of your hand. In Crane, you stare at a point in front of you to focus your Heart and Spirit. Without control of the gaze, there can be a disruption in the movement and thus a disruption of the posture, breaking concentration and losing the major benefits of each exercise.

## Breath

**Breath Matches the Movement:**
Each animal movement should coordinate the push and pull with the inhalation and exhalation. The most important part to pay attention to is the peak of the movement and inhaling into that. Once there, hold the breath until you feel discomfort.

**Maximum Inhalation During Animal Movement:**
During each animal movement, you inhale to your maximum capacity, but gently! It is important not to breathe in too much or else you will strain your lungs and do more harm than good. A good pointer is to breathe in until you feel full. Breathe in slowly so you can be more aware of your capacity, and never force the breath.

Breath holding is for people who do not have blood pressure problems. If you do not, make sure to hold the breath at the peak phase of each animal. Holding 3-9 seconds is a good base, and gradually build up from there if you can.

## Intention/Spirit

There are two parts you can pay attention to and I recommend one at a time:

1. The spirit of each animal: Each animal has a spirit; I am not talking about something esoteric, but more on the behavioral level. When we embody this animal, it can change

the way we perceive and interact with the world around us. In addition, it can greatly affect our emotions, and thus our organs.

2. The intention and sensation of the movement: Within each animal movement, focus on the natural expansive wave of inhalation to expand from within into the surrounding space. At the peak of the movement, we engage a 360° body-wide spacious expansion. This is done by gently engaging all the fascia at the same time. Through the rooting of the feet and the pull or push of the hands and arms, this engages all the superficial fascia, which envelops the body as a whole. Observe the feelings and sensations in your body. This has instant health benefits by dropping the endocrine stress levels. In some of the animals like Snake and Dragon, you will be able to engage in bi-directional movement, from hands to toes, meaning you will feel the hands moving in a different direction than the feet.

## Sequencing

The way in which the sequence is presented in this book is that you start with a high stance in relation to the others, which is Dragon. Progressively you go lower and lower into each animal. Tiger is lower than Dragon, Leopard is lower than Tiger and Snake is the lowest. Finally, you finish with a high stance such as in Crane. This is a standard sequence taught in most schools. When we use the Qigong exercises for Qigong prescriptions, we base the prescription on a 5 Element prescription model. Each animal fits with a different element of the 5 Elements as was presented earlier in this book. In order to be able to prescribe this Qigong, one has to become fluent in the 5 Elements and the 5 Element formula along with understanding this Qigong in depth. This is beyond the scope of this book as only a certified instructor or qualified teacher should be doing this. If you are interested in learning this 5 Element formula to be able to prescribe this Qigong for yourself and potentially one day for others, you must complete Levels 1, 2 and finally level 3 of our teacher training. For more information on our teacher trainings see here: *https://whitetigerqigong.com/qigong/teacher-certification/*

To find out when our next teacher training is please see our events page *whitetigerqigong.com/event*

## How I learned 5 Element Qigong

When I first found 5 Element Qigong, I had already developed a deep practice in Qigong so picking it up was quick. I had learned this Qigong in my early thirties, but then found 5 Element Qigong being taught in Wudangshan, which is one of the great major Taoist centers of the world. There it was being taught by a variety of teachers all using slightly different techniques. One of the more well-known sects teaching this is the San Feng Sect. It makes sense that the 5 Element Qigong sequences all looked different. as I studied under three different masters in Wudang Mountain; they all had the same teacher, yet their forms all look a little different although their underlying principles are generally the same. No two schools or teachers are identical. What became more interesting was when I met an old master (who I ended up studying with) who told me that his master had taught the lineage holder of a very well-known sect in Wudang Mountain a wide variety of forms. I had learned deeper secrets of this form outside of Wudang Mountain, coincidentally. The history of where this Qigong came from is a bit of a mystery. I have heard many debates as to the origin, but it is not my purpose to go into that in this book nor do I have an interest in the debate itself.

In China, there can be fierce debates as to who created certain Qigong forms and who "owns" them and who does not. I have no desire to get into those debates, since I feel this can harm the ability to spread a wonderful gift rather than promote getting together to share the beautiful knowledge. I don't claim to know everything about this Qigong and I know there are experts in it who know more about it than I do, but have not written books about it. What I do know is this Qigong is becoming more and more popular and this book was intended for my students, but I decided to also let it be public. As a person who believes in the evolution of Qigong, I am always seeking to advance these Qigong forms more and more as well as constantly seeking out experts and new perspectives to this day.

What is in this book may look different than what you see on videos or have been taught if you have learned this form. You can find a multitude of videos on this Qigong on YouTube (in English they call it 5 Animals Qigong), but on the Chinese videos on Youku (a Chinese video hosting website), they call it Wu Xing Qigong 无形气功。What is interesting is that in many of the videos the forms can look quite different. What is even more important to note is that what is often times taught at the schools is different from what is on the videos. Although I put the majority of the form in here, some of the deeper inner alchemy work should only be taught face-to-face as it can be dangerous to do otherwise without an experienced teacher to guide you. I have taken what I feel is the most effective way to do the animal movements from different teachers and integrated them into the forms you see here. I have also applied my understanding and studies of fascia and anatomy as well as having worked with fascia and anatomy experts to make the movements even more effective.

Since this knowledge is very special and powerful, not everything can be taught in books. Some secrets are reserved for in-person, verbal and physical transmission, and some secrets take many years of developing your character and worthiness before they can be revealed. There is great power in secrecy, and in the preservation of knowledge that deserves great respect. It is said by some that these teachings originated in Wudang Mountain Taoist Schools in China. Others claim it comes from different locations in China. The one fact we can prove now is that it is practiced all over the world. We are grateful for the knowledge of those ancestors and teachers who have passed this on.

五元氣功

# Qigong Theory

> "Wudang arts stress the movement of Qi and blood through the meridians. In training, one must reach a state of total relaxation. This is a cultivation process that takes a long time."
>
> *Taoist Hermit Guo Gao Yi*

## — General Concepts

### What is Qigong?

"Qi" (chee) means air or energy, while "gong" means work. Qi is defined as the circulating life force. In traditional Chinese culture, Qì (also chi or ch'i) is an active principle forming a part of any living thing. Qi is frequently translated as "life energy," "life force," or "energy flow." Qi is the central underlying principle in traditional Chinese medicine and martial arts. The literal translation of "Qi" is "breath", "air" or "gas." On a more profound level, Qigong is connected with the Tao (or Dao) which is the universal energy that comes from infinity and lives in infinity. It is the harmonizing of self with heaven and earth.

To put it simply, Qigong is an exercise and skill of harmonizing the spirit, body, and breath to achieve "oneness."

## Medical Qigong

The official definition of Medical Qigong in Chinese medical textbooks is the combination of Traditional Chinese Medicine theory applied to Qigong practice. Modern Medical Qigong utilizes not only Chinese Medicine Relationship theory, but also modern science and technology. It is an exciting and dynamic evolution, so let's dig deeper.

The word "medical" is self-explanatory. When you put them all together, Medical Qigong refers to the systematic application of energy in the body for health, healing and wellness purposes.

Medical Qigong exercises the internal and external body. Internal cultivation supports essence, Qi and spirit, while external cultivation supports sinew, bone and skin.

The use of Qigong as a medical therapy has been documented as far back as the ancient beginnings of Traditional Chinese Medicine. The branch of Qigong that is guided by Traditional Chinese Medicine theory is known as Medical Qigong.

Medical Qigong is a modality of Chinese Medicine. It is practiced in conjunction with acupuncture and herbal treatment, or strictly by itself. It is a method of moving Qi or energy through the meridians and organs of the body.

Medical Qigong has two parts: preserving health and treating illness. Medical Qigong is most optimally used as a preventative measure, but if illness has ensued, it is used to treat illness in a holistic way.

A form of Medical Qigong is Outgoing Qigong Therapy, in which the practitioner emits Qi to the patient to move stagnant energy or move Qi through the meridians and the organs. It is also often used in conjunction with acupuncture and herbs. To become a practitioner of Outgoing Medical Qigong Therapy, one must have a solid history of dedicated practice in Qigong and Medical Qigong theory to be able to generate the correct kind of Qi and direct it with precision. One of my Medical Qigong teacher's prerequisites for Medical Qigong was five years of Qigong experience. Outgoing Medical Qigong Therapy, however, is beyond the scope of this training and book.

Many Qigong documents have been discovered in ancient Chinese Medicine classic texts, such as the Yellow Emperor's Internal Classic, "Huang Di Nei Jing". It is interesting to note that, during the Sui Dynasty, Chao Yuan Fang, a well-known imperial physician, wrote a book on Medical Qigong, "General Treatise on Etiology and Symptomology of Various Diseases", which prescribes Qigong therapy for all diseases, instead of herbs. The traditional theory of Medical Qigong is built on the doctrines of Yin-Yang and the 5 Elements; the (Zang-Fu) Internal Organs and Meridians; Qi-Blood and Body Fluids; Jing (essence), Qi, and Shen.

Modern Medical Qigong is an assimilation of ancient Qigong methods. For example, Buddhists, Taoists and Confucianists all have their own healing Qigong methods. The modern methods are a synthesis of these methods for healing and nurturing a healthy life, rather than for spiritual enlightenment.

Taoist Qigong emphasizes the cultivation of both human life and spirituality. Traditional Chinese Medicine originates from Taoism itself. Taoism was the creator of the internal elixir, Qigong. I studied with a school of Taoists devoted to the development of the internal elixir practice. From Taoist Qigong also comes Zhou Tian, which means Heavenly Circulation, otherwise known as micro and macrocosmic orbit.

Buddhist Qigong is most well-known for the famous Iron Shirt Qigong of Shaolin, which is the intensive practice of making the body like steel. It was developed for martial arts purposes and is extremely powerful and effective.

Buddhist Qigong was originally more focused on spiritual enlightenment and martial protection, while Taoist Qigong believes the body and the spirit to be intrinsically connected. They believe to attain enlightenment you would need to cultivate a healthy and strong body. Most Buddhist Qigong forms were traditionally static, while Taoist had a broad range of dynamic and static. As Qigong evolves, it is more and more common to see dynamic Buddhist Qigong forms emerge.

What distinguishes Medical Qigong from the others is the special attention to the meridians and organs. A considerable amount of Medical Qigong is also adapted from Martial

Qigong, such as 8 Pieces of Brocade (Ba Duan Jin), which was created by Marshall Yue Fei. The 8 Pieces of Brocade has been a popular basic Medical Qigong set around China and the U.S. since the movements are easy to learn, but it is far from being most profound. There are sets of Medical Qigong that go much deeper into the body and stretch the body more significantly. It does not mean one is superior to another, but it is important to realize that Medical Qigong has many different forms, practices and levels.

Medical Qigong and Martial Arts Qigong have the same origins, but the intent and manner in which they are practiced are distinguishably different. Certain elements of Martial Arts Qigong can be found in most dynamic forms of Qigong.

## Dan Tian

In Chinese, the Dan Tian is the center and battery storage area of your life force. Many types of Taoist and Buddhist meditations and Qigong instruct the student to bring their attention or awareness to the Dan Tian, as it is believed to quiet the mind.

The Lower Dan Tian, otherwise known as the Xia Dan Tian, is translated as "elixir field," which lies three finger-widths below your navel and two finger-widths behind your navel, directly towards the center of your body. The two other Dan Tians are located at your third eye (Upper Dan Tian) area in the middle of your forehead, and your heart (Middle Dan Tian) area.

## Yin Yang

Yin and Yang rests on the belief that wholeness is composed in the union of opposites. They are both complementary and interdependent. Nothing is either all Yin or all Yang. Where there is light there is dark. Look at the Yin and Yang symbol, and you will see that each side is an inseparable part of the whole, while each contains part of the other. They create a continuous flow. In order to bring your body into balance you must balance your body's Yin and Yang. Yin and Yang principles will be discussed more thoroughly in the training and later in this book.

五元氣功

# 3 Treasures

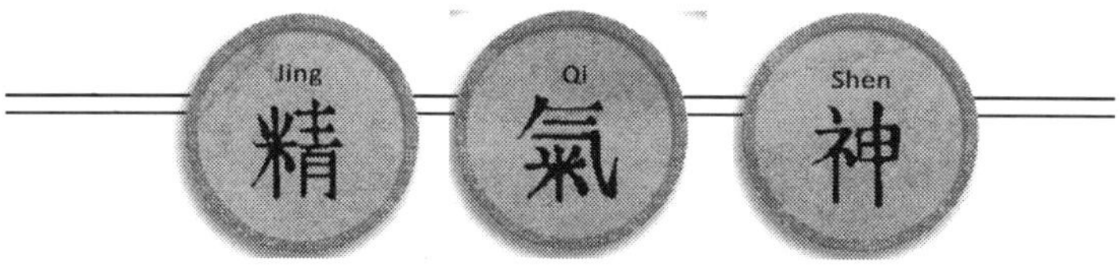


*In Chinese Medicine and Qigong there are 3 treasures that are to be guarded. In the Taoist schools of Qigong, Essence (Jing), Qi and Spirit (Shen) are taken as the original life drive and the material basis of life.*

## Jing

Jing is our life Essence. It corresponds to the physical self and the Earth. It determines how long you will live and it is your life force and is associated with your genetics. Our Jing can be depleted by life itself or exhausted by overwork, stress, and excessive emotions. It can also be replenished through certain types of Qigong and herbs.

## Qi

Qi is translated as vitality, although it is more complex than that. Qi is a refined and subtle substance but it can also be a functional activity of the organs in the body. Without Qi, we would not be able to move and we would die. There are different types of Qi, and Qi is sourced from two different places. The original Qi is inherited before your birth, while the second Qi is sourced from the air you breathe, liquids you drink and foods you eat. The original Qi is stored in your lower Dan Tian. This feeds the Jing of the five organs. The Qi you breathe, drink and consume is also stored in your lower Dan Tian.

The lower Dan Tian can warm the whole body or moisten the five Zang organs. The power of your metabolism also lies in the lower Dan Tian.

Focusing on your lower Dan Tian, the "fire" in your heart can descend and warm the "water" in your kidney. This helps maintain Yin essence. As fire generates earth (spleen), the Jing you have acquired is replenished.

## Shen

Shen is translated as the Spirit. When we practice Qigong, we also train the Shen or the mind. The practice of Qigong can calm the mind and spirit. It is said that a person with a strong Shen is intelligent, clear, centered, strong-minded, calm, and at peace. Qigong training will naturally calm and concentrate your mind and spirit by simplifying and purifying the mind and diminishing your desires. This will also contribute to keeping the mind tranquil while avoiding over-consuming the Shen. In Medical Qigong, they say "Don't seek fame or gain and pathogenic Qi will not be able to root itself deeply into your body." Regular Qigong practice can have profound effects on the mind and spirit.

The reason Qigong is so important is that it preserves, protects, replenishes, and supplies these 3 treasures. The Jing, Qi, and Shen work together, synchronized to produce the substances needed to stay youthful. The Jing is always controlled by the Qi; therefore, it is crucial to guard the Qi. The Shen is the ruler of the Jing and Qi, as it is the basis of the physical body and the foundation of the length of our life.

We refine the (Jing) essence and convert it into Qi, refining the Qi to nourish the (Shen) spirit, and refining the spirit to return to nothingness. You will find an exercise called Melting into Nothingness that we do at the end of our Qigong practice later in this book. This is the final process of returning the spirit into nothingness, or what we may call the cosmos.

# — How Qi Is Made

Qi is converted or made from essences within the body. Original Essence makes Water Qi. Essence from food and air makes Fire Qi. Practicing Medical Qigong helps convert the essence into Qi and helps make circulation more smooth and balanced.

**Qi can be stimulated through:**

1. Physical Movement
2. Mental Stimulation
3. Energizing the Shen - happiness or joy or even fear is an example.

Think about the last time you were really scared; did you feel tingly in your fight or flight mode? Qi was starting to flow. If you froze in fear, then the Qi was actually being pulled towards the center of your body and downwards. In this case, it is the opposite of fight or flight.

## Relaxation

Relaxation is one of the major goals and keys to success in Qigong for longevity. When the spirit and heart are relaxed, the body will relax. If the body can relax, the spirit and heart are more easily relaxed.

Physical Relaxation-being able to relax in a posture

**3 Levels of Relaxation**

1. Physical Relaxation: being able to relax in a posture
2. Relaxation of the muscles and meridians

3. Relaxation of the internal organs and finally the bones

In order to relax all 3 levels, we must first twist, pull and push the body while winding and unwinding the meridians, tendons, muscles and fascia surrounding the internal organs. Once we do this, we can more easily relax the spirit and emotional mind.

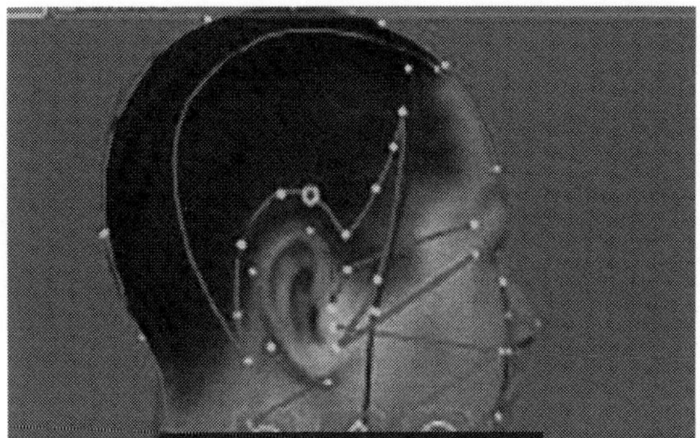

Relaxation of the muscles and meridians

During Organ Medical Qigong we lead the Five Qis to the Five Yin Organs. You can do this by sensing the organ. Once the organ is completely relaxed, you will be able to lead it more easily. Once you complete all of the 5 Element Qigong forms during your Zhan Zhuang, you lead the Qi to the organs in this order:

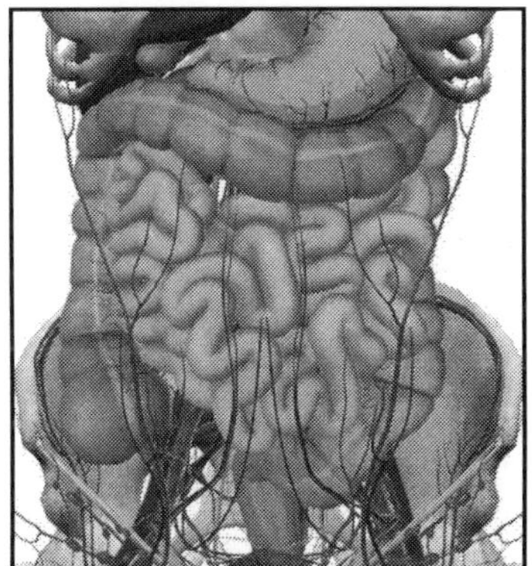

Relaxation of the internal organs and finally the bones

1. **Lungs** - easiest to sense
2. **Heart** - sense it beating
3. **Kidneys** - easier to sense than the liver and spleen because they contain liquid
4. **Liver** - this organ is bigger than the spleen so easier to sense
5. **Spleen**

五元氣功

# What Medical Qigong Can Treat

*Medical Qigong has been used throughout ancient and modern-day China to treat a wide variety of illnesses and diseases. It is often used in conjunction with Chinese Medicinal herbs, and is even used in Western medicine as a means of psychotherapy. Qigong, like psychotherapy, adjusts to the patient's mental state. Going beyond this, Qigong also adjusts the body and breath.*

Medical Qigong in China has been used for thousands of years, up to the present day, to treat various disorders such as: cancer (most types), sports injuries, gastrointestinal disorders, orthopedic disorders, broken bones, sprains, strains, common colds, arthritis, the flu, depression, attention deficit hyperactivity disorder, bipolar disorder, fibromyalgia, high blood pressure, nervous system imbalance and emotional disorders.

## What Qigong Cannot Treat

Although Qigong is used widely to treat a variety of ailments and diseases, in some cases it is best not used as primary therapy for the following disorders: parasites, bacterial infections, acute poisoning, radical physical trauma, bleeding, shock, severe organ diseases, serious mental illnesses and psychiatric disorders, such as severe schizophrenia, neurosis, mania and severe depression.

Qigong could, in fact, exacerbate some mental illnesses and psychological disorders and should be treated with caution.

## Who Can Learn Medical Qigong?

There are neither laws nor regulations on Medical Qigong. Anyone can practice Medical Qigong. China has only recently created a standardized Medical Qigong curriculum, but it is limited in scope and does not include many ancient Medical Qigong forms and exercises. A complete study would be almost impossible, due to the extent of Qigong taught throughout history.

The Medical Qigong principle rests on the fundamental belief that all illness arises from imbalance and stagnation in the "meridians," or energetic patterns in the body (see below for more on meridians). It is a preventative medicine used to treat various disorders by restoring and adjusting energetic balances, breaking through stagnation, and restoring unimpeded flow and circulation to the body.

Medical Qigong is becoming extremely important as healthcare costs continue to rise and economies shrink. People all over the world are waking up to the fact that they need to find alternative preventative medicine as a defense against the increasingly prohibitive cost of conventional medical care.

Medical Qigong is practiced by the healthy as well as those suffering from severe illnesses and diseases including cancer, sexual dysfunction, physical injury, and even common colds.

## Who can benefit from this Qigong?

Anyone can benefit from this Qigong. You don't have to have an illness, disease, or physical problems to benefit from Qigong. Qigong will improve performance for athletes, dancers, yoga students, martial artists, and even the high-level manager who requires intense focus and concentration. For these types of practitioners, it can help improve recovery times, heal muscle fascia, increase flexibility, improve concentration and more.

# — General Categories of Medical Qigong

The general categories of medical Qigong include Outgoing Qigong Therapy and Medical Qigong Exercises.

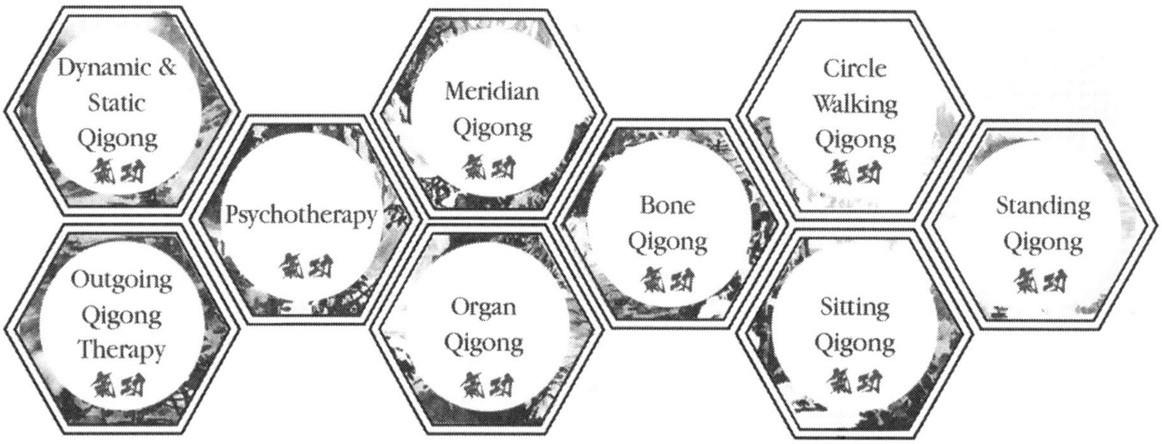


## Dynamic and Static Qigong

There are two main kinds of Qigong: Dynamic Qigong - Dong Gong (動功) Qigong - and Jing Gong Qigong (靜 功), or Static Qigong. Dynamic Qigong is simply Qigong in movement. It can be simple or complicated movements with deep twists, stances, and stretches and is considered more Yang. Static Qigong can be practiced standing, sitting, or lying down and is considered more Yin. Sitting is the most Yin practice, whereas dynamic, standing Qigong is the most Yang. In any complete system of Qigong, all three are studied and practiced. Additionally, within each practice, there is always a way to adjust your Yin and Yang.

動功

Dynamic Qigong

靜功

Static Qigong

Yin comes from stillness and Yang comes from motion. If Yin is in excess and Yang is deficient, it is best treated with more Dynamic Qigong. On the other hand, if Yang is in excess and Yin is deficient, it is best treated by practicing more Static Qigong. When motion reaches its extreme, Yin is produced, and when Yang reaches its extreme, Yin is produced. Finding the proper balance between Dynamic and Static Qigong is one of the keys to balancing Yin and Yang.

During menstruation cycles, when women need less Yang and more Yin; practices which produce Yang will encourage more blood flow, which is unnecessary in that situation. Meridian Medical Qigong exercises are designed to open up the meridian channels. The levels of Dynamic Medical Qigong Exercises include:

**1st level - Meridian Qigong or Jing Luo Gong**
**2nd level - Organ Qigong or Nei Zang Gong**
**3rd level - Bone Qigong or Gu Tou Gong**

In the first level of Medical Qigong, the practitioner needs to open the Meridian Channels of the body. Once you have opened the rivers (meridians), the next stage is to go deeper into the organs with Organ Qigong. Once you have opened and massaged the organs and meridians of the body, your body will be ready to go to a deeper level of Qigong with Bone Qigong. Bone Qigong requires a lot of flexibility and strength, as it has many deep stances and postures.

## Psychotherapy

As mentioned above, Medical Qigong can be used to regulate the mental state. This is done on a deeper level through the 3 Harmonies.

In Chinese Qigong, it is believed that the emotions can be regulated through regulating the body, breath, and mind. Each of the 5 Elements, which we will later explain in detail, is related to each of the five Yin Organs which are the heart, lungs, liver, spleen, and kidneys.

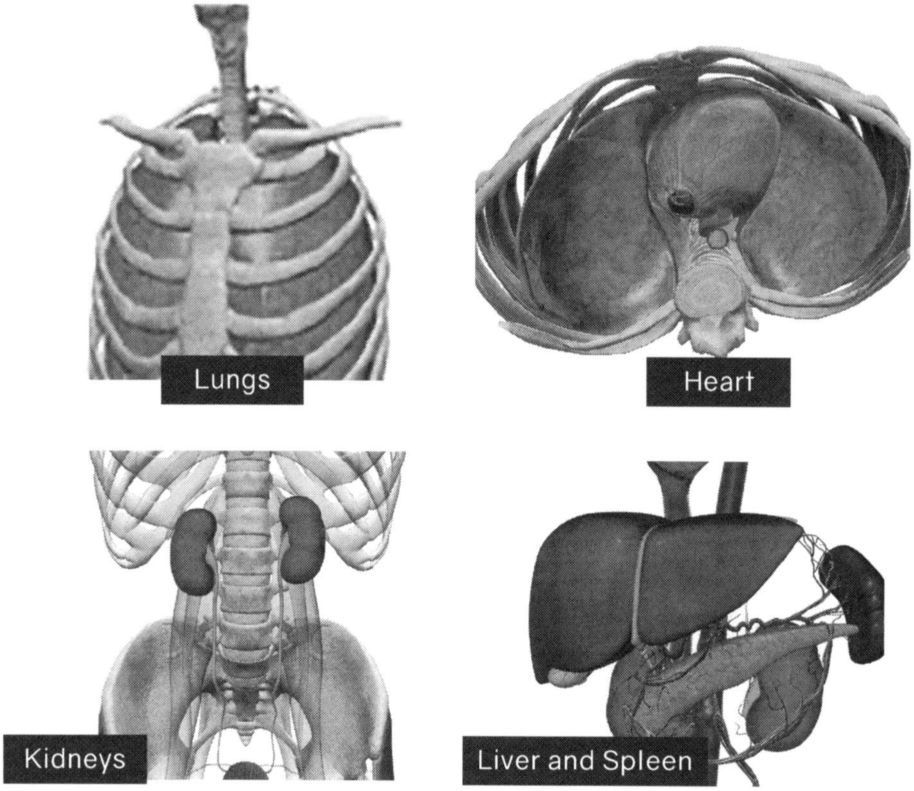


According to Chinese Medicine theory, each organ has a relationship with different emotions. When emotions are trapped inside the body they can negatively affect the related organ, further exacerbating the emotions. This can lead to emotional outbursts and even ultimately lead to serious diseases, such as cancer. By working on the emotions through Qigong exercises, one can literally squeeze the tension right out of the organs. This is how we can find a more balanced emotional state through Qigong. This concept will be explained in more details in the coming chapters.

## Meridian Qigong

In our Level One Medical Qigong course, we teach fundamental Meridian Qigong exercises. These Qigong exercises are comprised of various movements specifically designed to open the meridian pathways. This is a great foundation to any Medical Qigong or Qigong practice. Many practitioners use it as a warm-up preceding the more difficult Organ and Bone Qigong sets. Each exercise twists, stretches, pumps and pulses to move the Qi through one or more meridian pathways. These exercises will increase your flexibility, strength, and balance. Each movement requires you to explore a rhythm. We will explore meridians in more depth in later chapters.

## Organ Qigong

After opening the meridian pathways with Meridian Qigong exercises, the next step is to massage the internal organs with Organ Qigong. We teach a form comprised of eight Qigong exercises that gently massage your internal organs in multiple ways and angles through various twists and stretching movements, coupled with compression and expansion of the body.

## Bone Qigong

After mastering Organ Qigong and Meridian Qigong exercises, the next stage guides the Qi into the bone marrow, tendons and ligaments. Building upon the components and movements of the Meridian Qigong and Organ Qigong, the student is now ready to put the pieces together for the most profound Qigong experience possible. We teach a variety of Qigong exercises to do this, some of which are advanced forms that will challenge even the well-seasoned Qigong practitioner. This is an advanced stage of Medical Qigong which is more challenging than either Meridian or Organ Qigong, as it requires deep stances coupled with deep twisting movements.

Each of these sets feels different. If practiced together, you have the opportunity for maximum Qi development. This is a preventative medicine program that is free and can be practiced whenever and wherever you want.

White Tiger Qigong™ teaches forms that incorporate the bones, meridians and organs, such as the 5 Element Qigong and the 5 Animal Frolics, created by Hua Tuo. Hua Tuo was a pioneer in Medical Qigong practice and the creator of The Five Animal Frolics, which was the first series of dynamic Qigong documented in history.

## Circle Walking Qigong

I have a strong foundation in Baguazhang and I am a big proponent of the Circle Walking practice. Circle Walking is an ancient exercise of Taoist origin which has been taught to beginner and advanced students. In Medical Qigong Circle Walking the practitioner will learn the applications of Traditional Chinese Medicine theory to the practice.

Circle Walking involves having the practitioner hold various postures, including animal postures. Each posture opens different meridian pathways, massages internal organs, and will even drive Qi into the bone marrow with a deep walking posture.

With each carefully executed step, the practitioner is massaging the acupuncture points on the bottom of the feet. Coupled with special breathing and visualization techniques, it creates one of the most powerful Qigong experiences available. Some Qigong masters have said that Circle Walking is better than a hundred exercises. There are a number of Circle Walking practices which can be used for Medical Qigong purposes, martial arts, meditation and even spiritual practices.

## Sitting Qigong (Jing Zuo)

Sitting Qigong, such as Primordial Breathing with the Golden Elixir Breath, is used to treat a variety of gastrointestinal disorders and other illnesses. In traditional Qigong, the saliva is considered the Golden Elixir of health and vitality. The Taoists believe it has very powerful healing benefits.

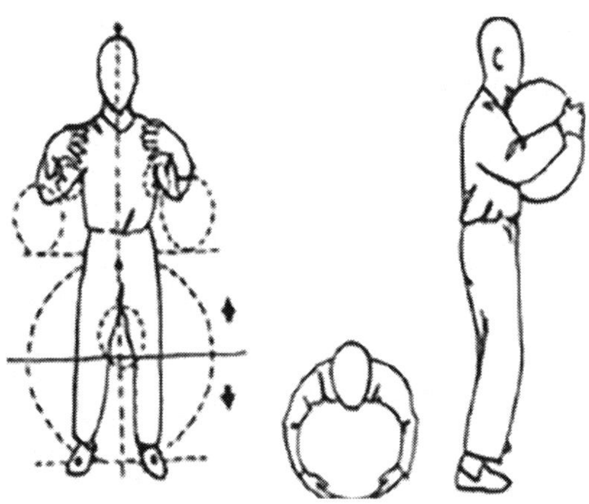

With Golden Elixir Qigong, you generate saliva in your mouth through chattering the teeth multiple times and then swirling your tongue around your mouth multiple times. Then you swallow a small portion of it, coordinated with the inhalation and exhalation. It can aid in problems related to digestive issues, excessive heat, and much more. Chinese Jing Zuo medical Qigong sitting practices include Primordial Breathing (Tai Xi), otherwise known as Fetal Breathing or Embryonic Breathing, which involves the Golden Elixir method of swallowing saliva to improve digestion, cool fire in the body, and many more.

## Standing Qigong (Zhan Zhuang)

Zhan Zhuang, or Standing Qigong, is literally translated as "standing like a post." This Qigong training routine is also sometimes translated as "standing-on-stake," "standing Qigong," "standing like a tree," "post-standing," and "pile-standing." Standing Medical Qigong is used in both martial and medical Qigong to help balance the central nervous system. There are many kinds of Zhan Zhuang postures. The most common being to place the feet about shoulder-width apart with the knees slightly bent and the sacrum pulling downwards. There are also several general hand and arm postures. Zhan Zhuang can be used with various animal postures for different effects on the various meridians and organs.

The main goals are centering the body between heaven and earth. Rooting into the earth through the feet and connecting to the heavens through the crown point of the head, your spine lengthens and your place is found between heaven and earth. Standing Medical Qigong also helps you in practicing the proper back posture before going into dynamic exercises. Despite having no recognizable external movements, this type of Qigong is a highly energetic exercise system. Zhan Zhuang, unlike other methods, develops internal energy efficiently instead of consuming it.

Those unfamiliar with this Medical Qigong can experience severe muscle fatigue and subsequent trembling at first. But once sufficient stamina and strength have been developed, the practitioner can work on developing "Zhong Ding" or the central equilibrium and sensitivity to specific areas of tension in the body.

Standing Qigong is often used to remove blockages in Qi flow. With correct practice, blockage removal occurs and has a normalizing effect on the body. The body regains its natural ability to function optimally when habitual tension or tissue shortening (or even lengthening) is normalized. It is thought that a normalized body might also prevent muscular and skeletal health problems. When practiced to develop relaxed postures, Zhan Zhuang has a beneficial calming effect. While doing Standing Qigong you can become keenly aware of any tight areas or tension in the body. Once found, you can relax those areas through various breathing techniques and intentions.'

## — Which Style is Right for Me?

By experiencing each style, you will discover the right one for you. It may be one or all of the above-mentioned styles of Medical Qigong. They can be practiced in conjunction with one other and are all worth exploring.

Sometimes just one or two exercises from a single category of Qigong will be prescribed to a patient, while others might want to master the whole system. Some Qigong forms, such as one of the Meridian forms, will be more challenging to those with balancing difficulties while others, such as Organ Qigong, will be more challenging to those with a stiff back.

I highly recommend you incorporate a daily Medical Qigong routine into your schedule as a potent form of natural preventive medicine.

## — Energy Stagnation and Disease

In Taoism, it is believed that the human form is a microcosm of nature. As such, the Chinese say that the meridians are like the rivers that flow to the oceans and lakes of your body, the oceans and lakes of your body being your organs.

Naturally, if a river is blocked, stagnation may result. If it cannot find a way to flow over time, it will eventually burst or find an alternative route that may negatively alter the course of nature. Likewise, in the human body if meridians are blocked, the proper nutrients, oxygen and Qi cannot flow to the organs, resulting in stagnation and consequently, disease.

This energy blockage is tantamount to cutting off the oxygen supply to your organs; they cannot breathe properly, and therefore suffer. If they suffer for too long, they can become damaged. It is therefore imperative to keep the body's meridian channels open and flowing.

## Removing Stagnation with Qigong by Pulsing

To break through stagnation, we need to create a pulse of energy. The greater the blockage, the stronger the pulse needs to be. Pulsing is done by coordinating breath with intention and movements in dynamic Qigong.

Even the movements in our Bagua Organ Qigong set are done with wave-like motions to help the pulse. Many physiological and kinesiological processes in the body occur in waves, from the light waves that stimulate the retina through vision to the pulsing waves of the blood in the arteries and veins.

Breathing into the Dan Tian is done when inhaling, guiding the energy with intent into the palms and/or feet upon exhalation.

All the meridian pathways end in the feet and the hands (aside from the two extra channels which run along the spine and front). By focusing on a rhythmic pulse from your Dan Tian to your extremities, the Qi will naturally flow like water through your meridians from your Dan Tian. This will bring circulation through the meridians. Done in conjunction with the movements, a strong Qi flow throughout the body is created.

Pulsing is also done with the third eye and Dan Tian in Primordial Breathing Qigong. Primordial Breathing will be explained in a later book as it is beyond the scope of this one.

Once all these centers are coordinated with the breath and movement, you will be able to generate a strong pulse of energy through the meridian pathways to the extremities. This is practiced with the Four Gate Breathing Method.

During Qigong practice, eight pulses are commonly recognized. These are the foundational pulses, but many more variations can be experienced. Research has shown that hotness is most common, second to automatic muscle contraction which is usually followed by the other senses or pulses.

Different Qigong forms will likely induce different pulses. For example, Circle Walking can induce a feeling of floating, while some Bone Qigong forms will feel heavy, hardening and contracting. A myriad of sensations and pulses are possible, but it is best for the practitioner to experience theirs without the preconceived notion of others' experiences. Once you have the pulsation, observe it and then allow it to run its own course without intervention.

**THE EIGHT PULSES**

1. Contraction
2. Stretching
3. Coolness
4. Hotness
5. Floating
6. Sinking
7. Hardening
8. Softening

五元氣功

# The Three Harmonies

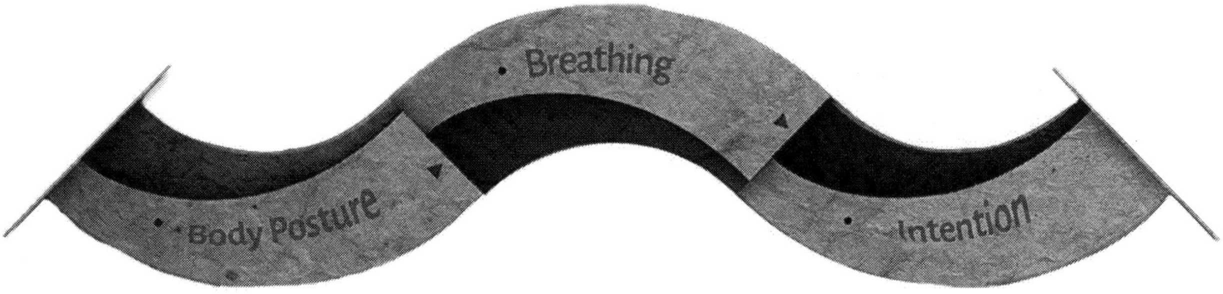


*Proper posture is the foundation of all Qigong practice. A student once asked while I was teaching on the first day of her class, "Where should I be guiding the Qi?" I told her that she must first learn the form and postures properly before I would show her where to guide the Qi. She became adamant and refused to do the form unless I told her where her Qi was flowing. Patiently, I explained to her that before you can even think about guiding the Qi, you must have correct form. Without proper posture, you will not open up the proper channels.*

Once you have the correct form, you add the breath. The breath is a major component of guiding Qi. You should focus on allowing the breath to guide the movement and not the other way around. The breath usually matches an exhalation with the stretch and an inhalation on the relaxing part of the movement.

Once you can get the breath and the form harmoniously synchronized, it is time to add the visualization of guiding the Qi. When I first begin teaching Qigong to new students, I don't like to tell them which exercises are related to which meridians because they want to bypass the first two stages and go directly to visualization. This is due to lack of patience and understanding of the importance of posture and breath. In my years of Qigong experience, I have found that the benefits come not through focusing on the meridians themselves, but from focusing on the feet and hands with the exhalation as all the meridian channels run through these spots anyway. Once you realize the proper posture, you will also be able to feel the meridians opening. This can take time for many people because they are not used to sensing different layers of their body.

If you only focus on guiding the Qi through the meridians, you may not be able to relax, which is a major objective in Qigong. Stress stifles Qi flow.

## — Adjusting the Body

Before we even begin to think about practicing Qigong, we must adjust the body into the proper posture and movement.

One of the fundamental postures of our system is the alignment of the perineum (Hui Yin) with the earth and the Crown Point (Bai Hui) with the sky. This creates a natural alignment with heaven and earth.

If you imagine a ball hanging from a string, gravity naturally pulls it down. Your body is the same, in that the Dan Tian is the ball naturally hanging down from the string, which gives you a naturally straight spine. This posture creates the perfect connection between heaven and earth, and our body is the ideal conduit. Throughout all of the turns and twists in the exercises, try to maintain this connection between heaven and earth. Of course, some exercises require that you bend down, but in every upright exercise, maintain this principle of posture.

The dynamic movement is important in Qigong as it helps increase stability, flexibility, strength, and mobility of the joints. Correct dynamic movement in Qigong exercises the limbs and bones of the exterior of the body and stimulates the Five Zang and Six Fu organs in the interior. This harmonizes the internal and external body. It also harmonizes the lower and upper body, which leads to a holistic form of healing and exercise.

# Adjusting the Breath

Once we have adjusted the body into the correct posture and/or form, then we must adjust the breath. The White Tiger Qigong™ System has 64 breathing techniques. In actuality, it has eight foundational breathing techniques that eventually combine to create 64 total techniques. Here are some basic techniques:

Normal Abdominal

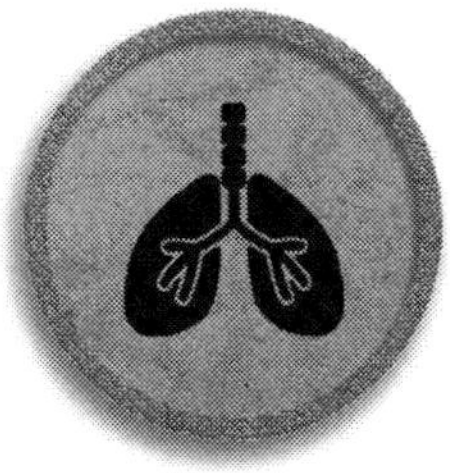
Holding Breath

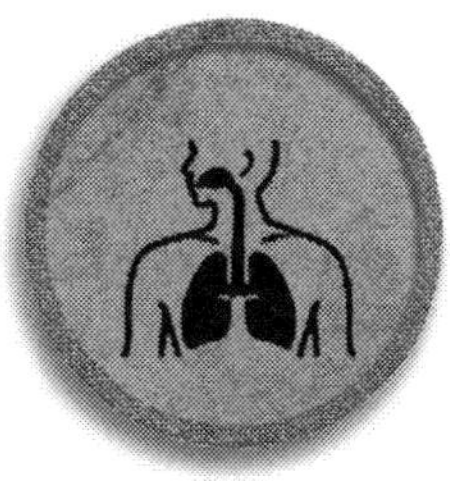
Reverse Breathing

Four Gate Breathing

## Normal Abdominal

Abdominal diaphragmatic breathing will lower the blood pressure, activate peristalsis, and increase the venous return of oxygenated blood. This also increases the overall oxygen level of the blood. It also draws the Qi down into the lower part of the body which helps to relax the mind. Focused lower belly breathing will also strengthen the kidneys and the Ming Men Fire (the kidneys in Traditional Chinese Medical theory are the activating yang element for the spleen and the lungs, thereby activating the digestive and respiratory systems).

## Reverse Breathing

Conversely, active breathing focused in the upper chest will increase blood pressure and stimulate the heart and lungs to move the blood and Qi more quickly and with greater force throughout the body. For people with low blood pressure and mental dullness due to sluggish circulation of blood and Qi, this can be very helpful.

Holding Breath in China is called Biqi Fare Fa (闭气发热法), which means "*Holding Qi to produce Heat Method*". This method is used as the practitioner inhales and then holds the breath to produce heat. It is used in conjunction with the perception of heat and fire developing. There are many methods of breath holds. These are generally taught to intermediate and advanced practitioners, so beginners are not advised to practice holding their breath without personal instruction from an experienced teacher.

闭气发热法

Holding Breath

## Four Gate Breathing

Four Gate Breathing Qigong has been used throughout history in Chinese Qigong in both Martial and Medical Qigong. In Martial Qigong, it is primarily used for energizing the hands and feet for martial power. It is also used as a sensory method, as the more you do the Four Gate Breathing, the more sensitive you become in "listening" to energy. In Medical Qigong, it is used to create circulation throughout the meridians and the body as the twelve main meridians all come out into the feet and hands.

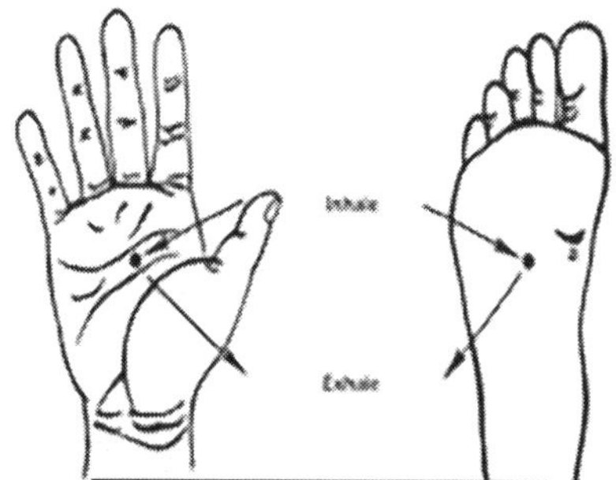

Diagram 2: Lao Gong and Yong Quan points

Medical Qigong practitioners who practice Outgoing Qigong emitting therapies focus on the Two Gates in the palms and practice this to gain greater ability to draw the Qi to their palms and fingertips for outgoing healing. The Two Gates are also used to sense the patient's energy. The more the breathing is practiced, the more sensitive your hands will become.

Breathing should naturally inhale into the Dan Tian and exhale into the Four Gates: the palm centers (Lao Gong points) and the center of the bottom of the feet (Yong Quan points). The Yong Quan points are called the "Bubbling Wells," as it is believed that Qi springs from them like water from a well. By breathing from the Dan Tian and to the extremities, you are creating a pulse of Qi. By coordinating the movements with the breath, you are creating a stronger pulse.

This is why it is so crucial to create a rhythm, as a rhythmic pulse will flow stronger than a broken one. In most cases, the exhalation will match with the stretch or outward movements, while the inhalation will match the expansion of the chest.

Four Gate Breathing can be done lying down, standing, or sitting. If done sitting, do not sit cross-legged as this can stifle the Qi flow to the legs. It is usually best done sitting on the edge of a chair, or with the legs straight out in front of the body. The Four Gate Breathing has a Fire Method and a Water Method, which will be described in the next sections.

## Four Gate Breathing Visualization Keys

Create a pump from the Dan Tian to the part of the body that is being stretched, all the way to the extremities. We do this through correct breathing techniques coupled with correct visualization:

- Inhale to the Dan Tian
- Exhale to the extremities or part being stretched

The purpose of this pump is to break through stagnation in the meridians. The easiest way to do this is to send Qi from the Dan Tian to the four extremities (hands and feet).

In order to understand how the Qi is flowing, you should study the Meridian Maps. Do not intentionally try to move Qi through actual single Meridian points. Unless you are a very well-trained Qigong practitioner of many years and have absolutely no distractions, it is easy for Qi to get stuck in the meridian points, or worse, create Rising Qi to the head.

**CHALLENGE**

Try to do at least a hundred Four Gate Breaths per day. While going to sleep, count your breaths until you fall asleep. On many occasions, I have fallen asleep while doing the Four Gate Breathing, only to wake up later feeling intensely strong vibrations of energy in my limbs and Dan Tian.

Symptoms of Rising Qi can be mild to severe headaches and dizziness. The safest and best way to do visualization is simply to pay attention to the Dan Tian area upon inhalation and focus on the hands and feet upon exhalation. The Qi will naturally move through the meridians on its own.

## The Yin and Yang of Breath

We must understand the Yin and Yang of the breath. The act of inhalation is Yin, as we are drawing energy inwards. The act of exhaling is Yang, as we are sending energy outwards. Think of physical exertion and the coordination of an exhale. The effect of inhalation on the body is Yang as we are drawing in energy. When we exhale, it has a Yin effect on the body as we are dispersing energy. Death is going back to the ultimate Yin state. Think of a diver, who must breathe in to have the energy to dive for a while. They must breathe out and then in again or else they will drown. Before drowning, they would breathe out all their air, which is Yin.

You can further adjust the body's Yin and Yang by adjusting the respiration rate. Breathing faster is Yang, while breathing slower is Yin.

Research has shown that prolonged exhalation can stimulate the parasympathetic nerves, resulting in a slower heart rate, lower blood pressure, increased salivary secretion and faster gastrointestinal peristalsis.

Once you grasp the concept of the Yin and Yang of breath you can further regulate the body's water and fire.

Breathing during Qigong practice serves not only to strengthen the respiratory system, but also to improve digestion, the nervous system and the cardiovascular system.

# — Adjusting the Spirit

Adjusting the spirit consists of using our intention to guide our focus to the purpose of the exercise and visualization to guide our imagination. The purpose is to perceive what we are visualizing and to "feel it". For example, in Dragon Ball Qigong at the end of the book, you will try to visualize a ball, not only seeing the image of a ball, but more importantly trying to feel it.

意

Intention

**Intention** (Yi) 意, is a condition of purposeful being and a state of allowing. It gives energy direction.

## How do you create intention in Qigong by simply being aware?

If you want to bring Qi to your hands, just become aware of your hands. If you want to create fiery hot Qi feelings in your hands, then see it in your mind. You do not think about it; it is just a state of being. If you think the thought "I want to put Qi in my hands," then you are in your head and will create rising Qi.

Try putting your mind's eye in your hands when projecting your Qi into your hands. For example, if you want to throw a ball to a friend then you just do it, you don't think about it. It is the same with Qigong, don't think about it, just do it. I know one high-level Qigong master whose healing touch feels like needles are coming from his fingers into your body—and he isn't even touching you. When I asked him his secret, he said that it is just his intention. He said that it came very naturally as he "just did it." He told me that if I continued to practice the way I had been, the intention would grow stronger and stronger until it manifests itself.

That is why so few people can achieve such incredible results with Qigong; they don't have the patience or the time to strengthen their intention through long-term practice. Granted, this master is over 55 years old, but he had a lifetime of just practice.

Your Xin 心, which is your heart, affects your intention. If you are practicing Qigong and your intention is to send Qi to your limbs, but you have anger inside, that anger will be directed into your body. That is why we have the fire method to expel anger (explained later in the book). If you are practicing, but in your heart you do not believe in Qigong, it will affect your intention. It is best to start Qigong with a clear, calm mind so you do not direct negative energy in the body or to others. You must have a calm and clear mind and heart.

As a beginning practitioner, I suggest you stick with simple intentions, such as the intention to generate the pulse from the Dan Tian to the limbs during dynamic forms of Qigong and especially when doing Four Gate Breathing. Once you can do that, add more complex intentions of hot and cold, etc.

When doing static Qigong, the way you concentrate the energy can determine the amount of Yin and Yang. Dynamic mind concentration is associated with Yang, while static mind concentration is more Yin. For example, if focusing on the Dan Tian you can spin a ball inside it, this is more Yang, while having a still ball is more Yin.

Synchronizing intention or visualization with inhalation and exhalation, finally coupled with movement, is what makes Dynamic Qigong, Qigong.

Without intention or visualization, it would merely be an exercise. Intention tells the Qi where to go. The breath and movement help move the Qi through different muscle fibers, organs, tendons, and ligaments.

The Qi follows the Yi 意 (intention) and the blood follows the Qi, thus stimulating maximum circulation while simultaneously concentrating and calming the spirit.

## The 3 Results

The following is an example of how to combine intention with breath and movement. Let's say you have a movement that is pushing forward. When you push, imagine you are pushing something heavy like a car or pushing through water. This visualization will stimulate the mind to send blood and Qi to that area when you are able to do this while maintaining a loose and relaxed posture.

Generally, we exhale while we push and inhale coming back to center. If you were really pushing a car, you would exhale as you push; thus, the mind is naturally molded to respond by sending blood and circulation to that area.

## Putting It All Together

The right posture and movement in harmony with your breath and your Yi ⊠ (intention) lead the Qi flow, and where the Qi goes the blood flows. On every inhalation, you draw the focus back to your Dan Tian, and on every exhalation, you lead the Qi to the extremity or the part of the body that you are moving. The reason for this is that we want to create a habit of a natural pump with the breath and the mind to circulate the Qi and blood throughout the meridians. The 12 main meridians all end in the limbs, so focusing on the exhalation means the Qi and blood will naturally flow through them.

There is actually no need to focus on the meridians themselves, as Qi and blood flow like water, finding the easiest pathway. This is why posture and proper body alignment are so important in these exercises, as you are sending a flow through the proper meridians.

In many of the White Tiger Qigong™ exercises, you create a flow of Qi from your Dan Tian (an area of the solar plexus) to your extremities and back to your Dan Tian.

Each exercise has a stretch that reaches its limit so that the movement helps guide the Qi there. In the beginning, you must focus on correct form, next add the breath, and finally the visualization (of color, for example). Without these 3 Adjustments, it is not Qigong, just exercise. Learn the 3 Adjustments for each Qigong exercise one at a time and eventually combine them. Some Qigong exercises focus more on one of the 3 Adjustments than others. For example, Dragon Ball is more focused on form and visualization while simply using a relaxed and natural method of breathing.

The 3 Adjustments all affect each other. Using visualization can calm and focus the spirit, thereby changing the rate of respiration. The rate of respiration can change the physiological state of the body. The 3 are intertwined and have a rhythmic influence upon each other. Practice them separately and then unify them until there is no separation of them.

Once a practitioner becomes advanced, they do not need to make any adjustments because it starts to happen naturally as it becomes second nature.

Once the Spirit, breath, and body are unified, you reach the Taoist state of unification of the macrocosm, which is the unification of Heaven, human, and Earth - "天人合一" -, which means Heaven and human are one.

天人合一

Heaven and human are one

## The 3 Harmonies and Its Applications for Medical Qigong

The results of all this are simple. In Medical Qigong we say, "Where the intention (Yi 意) goes the Qi goes, where the Qi goes, the blood flows." In Martial Qigong we say, "Where intention (Yi 意) goes, the Qi goes, and where the Qi goes, the force (Li ⊠) goes."

According to Chinese Medicine Theory, the heart (心) governs the Spirit and is the master of the five Zang organs and the six Fu organs. Adjusting the Spirit can calm the emotional mind and bring balance to the nervous system, thus regulating the Qi in the organs as well as the whole body. Try to recall a scary situation that really startled you. Your whole body tensed, your heart beat dramatically increased and you probably lost a sense of your increased breathing rate. You had, in a sense, lost voluntary control over your body as instincts kicked in. Now this can be a very good thing in survival situations; the problem is that we put ourselves in these types of situations daily, through severe stress from work and life. As the world appears to be becoming increasingly chaotic, it is more crucial than ever to learn to adjust the Spirit, body, and breath.

Only when we are in a relaxed state, with the body becoming more open and fluid and the breath relaxed and/or controlled, are we setting ourselves up for a state of healing.
In order to reach these states, the practitioner must believe. Without belief, the results will be weak if any. People ask me all the time:

*"Do you think I can heal my illness with this Qigong?"*

I respond, "More importantly, do you believe you can heal yourself with this Qigong?"

五元氣功

# Meridians, Modern Research & the Muscle Fascia

*As Qigong goes through a modern evolution, much research has and is being conducted to improve Medical Qigong's efficacy through using insights from modern medicine and scientific research. As my master told me, he always wished his students would evolve the existing Qigong. This is why I have delved deeply into fascia research and sports science. I have gained incredible insights and breakthroughs that I am sharing with you.*

There has been ongoing research into physically identifying where the meridian systems actually are in the body. In his ground-breaking book "Anatomy Trains"[1], Thomas Meyers dissected cadavers to understand the inner workings of the muscle fascia. He discovered previously unknown lines of muscle fascia interwoven throughout the body. He called these connections The Myofascial Meridians. At the time, he was neither looking for nor referring to the Asian Meridian system. It was only later that he realized the uncanny parallels of the meridian lines in Traditional Chinese Medicine to his own discovery of these Myofascial Meridian lines.

On a simple level, muscle fascia can be defined as the dense fibrous connective tissue that interpenetrates and surrounds the muscles, bones, nerves, and blood vessels of the body.

[1] Anatomy Trains: Myofascial Meridians for Manual and Movement Therapists, by Thomas Meyers

Meyers explains that fascia is the biological fabric that holds us together. You are about 70 trillion cells all humming in relative harmony; fascia is the 3-D spider web of fibrous, gluey, and wet proteins that hold them all together in their proper placement. Understanding fascia is essential to the dance between stability and movement – crucial in high performance, central in recovery from injury and disability, and ever-present in our daily life from our embryological beginnings to the last breath we take.

What Meyers explains is his belief that the Western anatomy perspective of individual muscles is not true. He believes that we don't have 600 muscles; we actually have one muscle within 600 fascial pockets. This would confirm the Chinese belief that blockages in one meridian line can affect other meridians as well.

There is conclusive evidence that the fascial net responds and distributes forces as a whole, not just locally. This was exemplified when strain was measured in various tissues while doing the straight leg lift test, commonly thought to measure hamstring resistance to hip flexion (a movement we have in one of the Meridian Qigong exercises). It was discovered that the strain distributes itself throughout the myofascial net.

According to Meyers, the distribution tracks the Superficial Back Line, the Spiral Line, and the Back Functional Line. The Superficial Back Line is related to the Bladder Meridian. The Spiral Line is related to the Stomach and Bladder Meridians of the acupuncture Meridians from Traditional Chinese Medicine.

Modern research has shown the link in both form and function between the workings of acupuncture and the fascial network in general. Prominent acupuncturist and researcher, Dr. Helene Langevin, has shown that connective tissue along with collagen fibers and fibroblasts wind around the end of an acupuncture needle when it is rotated in place, creating detectable mechanical effects. Dr. Langevin concluded that oriental acupuncture meridians may follow intermuscular or intramuscular fascial planes.

Meyers quotes Osteopath Phillip Beach, from his book[2]: *"In essence it is hypothesized that the Chinese mapped the minimum number of lines, in exactly the right location,*

[2] Muscles and Meridians: The Manipulation of Shape by Phillip Beach

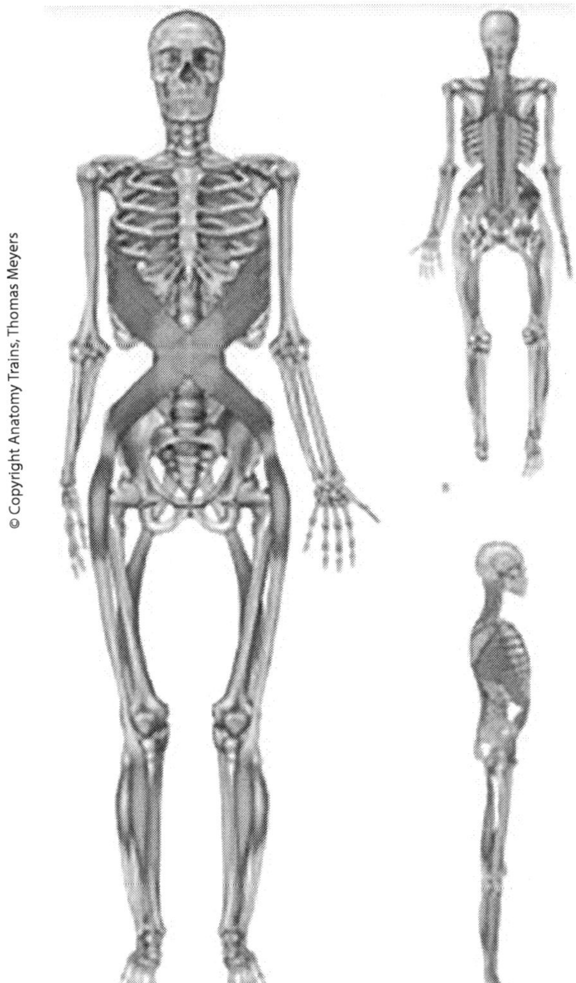


Spiral Line[3]

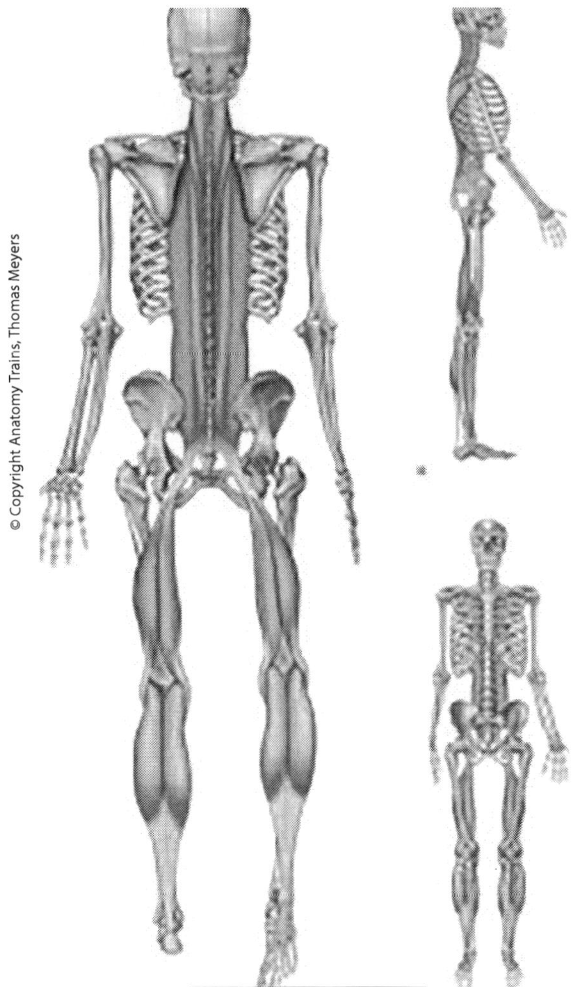


Superficial Back[3]

*to accurately/predictably control subtle human shape in three dimensions. Shape and function are usually correlated."*

Meyers believes that 'shape control' might be the guiding principle that unites the signaling response through the connective tissue and the odd but intuitively apt course of the meridian lines across the body.

This explains why, through proper manipulation of the fascia, you can relieve headaches and heal muscle injuries and more. It is a very exciting time as the connections of modern scientific research and the meridians are taking a whole new dimension.

[3] Reprinted from Anatomy Trains: Myofascial Meridians for Manual and Movement Therapists, 3E, Thomas Meyers, 2014, with permission from Elsevier

One of the greatest joys and fascinating aspects of Qigong for me was the discovery of the connections within my body. As a young student, I thought it rather mystical to feel these connections, but as I began to study Western anatomy I realized I was in fact feeling the connections of the muscle fascia throughout my body. My discovery of Thomas Meyer's work and others helped to confirm evidence of what I had known all along. It is one thing to read about the meridians, but to feel and experience these connections takes patience and lots of practice and the rewards are immeasurable.

When training the animal movements, aim to feel the pull and stretch along these meridian lines from your fingertips to your toes in the direction of the line, in order to truly experience the stretch.

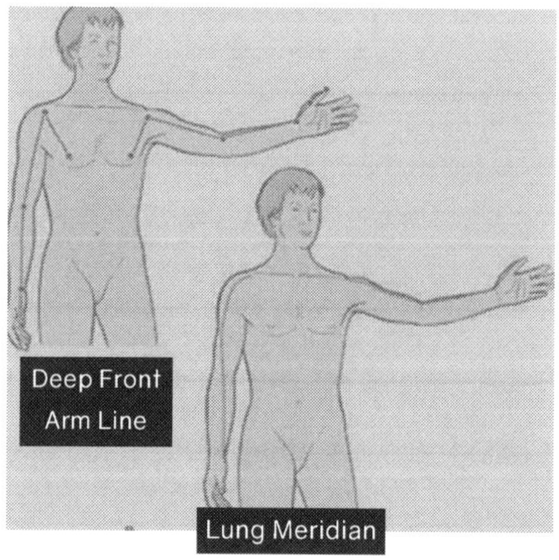


To allow the myofascial chains to work in the best possible way and enable movement, the trunk must be stabilized. We do this through the stances, which stabilize the trunk in the 5 Element Qigong. In the Bagua Organ Qigong, this is done through a solid horse stance.

Imagine right now you are wearing a suit. Your skin is your suit. Underneath your skin, you have layers of other clothing which are your deeper layers of fascia. They move against one another, sliding, pulling and stretching as well as contracting. Now imagine you can change the shape of your suit. You can have a tight suit, loose suit, relaxed and supple suit, or a strong suit. What kind of suit do you want?

This Qigong system creates what we call the "Bamboo Body". It is strong, yet flexible, supple and elastic. Think of the bamboo tree, it moves with the wind, yet stays rooted and firm. You can bend it very far and it will snap right back with high elasticity. Why wouldn't you want to make this kind of suit?

Your fascia, nervous system and self-image are being remodeled. By practicing the 5 Element Qigong, you are remodeling your whole self with a new way to move and hold yourself; thus, you change the way you perceive yourself and your relationship with the world.

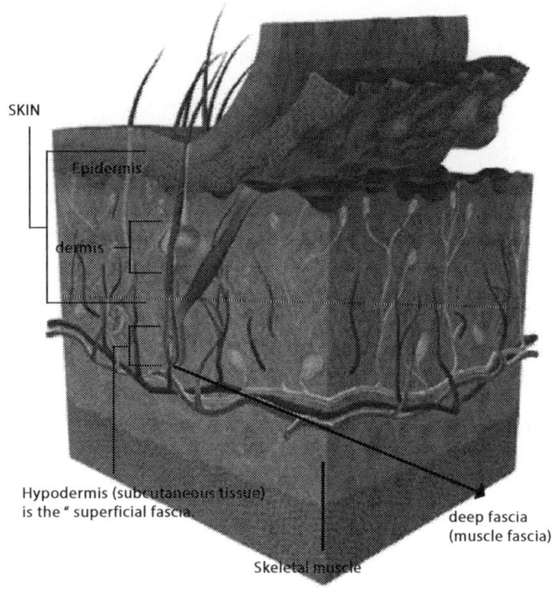


Fascia provides structural and functional continuity between the body's hard and soft tissues. It is a ubiquitous elastic–plastic, sensory component that surrounds, supports, separates, connects, divides, wraps, and gives both shape and functionality to the rest of the body, while allowing gliding, sliding motions, as well as playing an important role in transmitting mechanical forces between structures.

The twisting, compression and expansion of the visceral fascia helps release tension and blockages in the fascia.

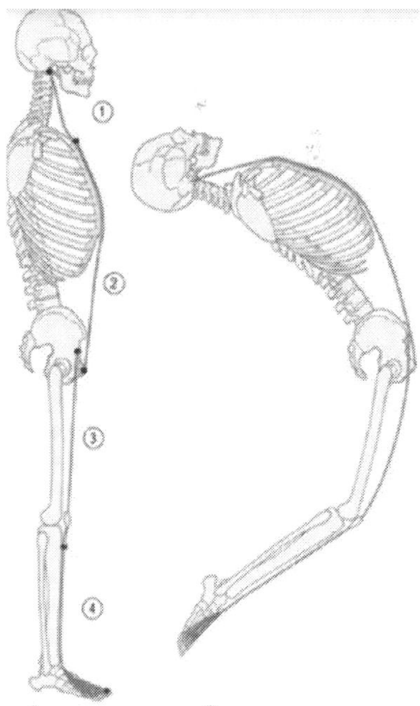

[4]

Loading, stretching or compressing will inevitably squeeze water from the sponge-like connective tissues. Once that is done, it may be replaced with fresh fluid from surrounding tissue and the local vascular network. This is what my master was referring to when he told me that, in our Qigong, we are squeezing out our organs and wringing out the meridians, and when we go into the expansion phase we let fresh, healing Qi in.

The fascial web can be seen as our largest sensory organ in terms of overall surface area. With regards to the sheer quantity and richness of nerve endings, this network can

[4] Reprinted from Anatomy Trains: Myofascial Meridians for Manual and Movement Therapists, 3E, Thomas Meyers, 2014, with permission from Elsevier

'match' our sense of sight, not to mention hearing or any of our other normal sensory organs.

The problem with many stretching routines and similar forms of exercise is that they focus on linear movements when, in actuality, the fascia needs movements on multiple planes. Apart from the rectus abdominis, very few tissues in the body (bone, muscle, and ligament) are actually linear. White Tiger Qigong™ aligns with the body's natural way of moving.

According to sports science principles, Qigong is considered a form of dynamic stretching. Long-term and regular use of such dynamic stretching, correctly performed, can positively influence the architecture of the connective tissue, in that it becomes more elastic. The elasticity of the fascial tissue is the key to its high capacity to store kinetic energy. I believe this is the Qi that the fascia can contain. This is crucial for dancers and athletes as much as for the regular ol' Joe.

Scientific studies have shown a higher output of power from myofascial tissues due to their more elastic recoil properties than muscle. This is significant for martial artists, dancers and athletes as they search for the best training methods to generate power.

What is also interesting is that the elasticity of the fascial elements reduces the work needed from active muscle fibers, which leads to a decrease in energy expenditure. I believe this is what my master was referring to when he told me that when you use Qi, you don't need muscle energy and you will have increased stamina.

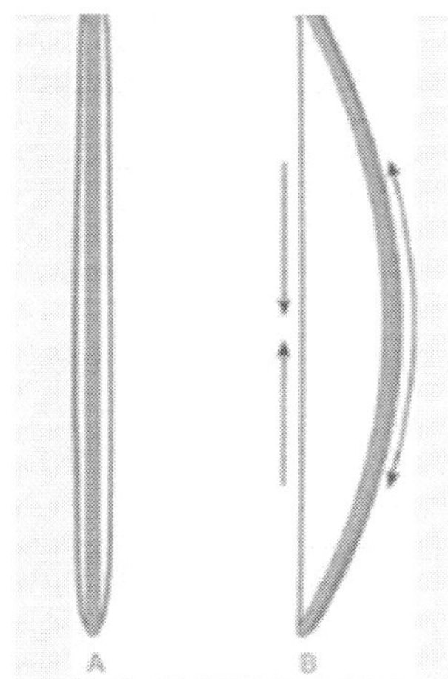


It is important to keep the fascia flexible. The storage of elastic energy is only possible in more flexible tissues. Due to the superior muscle tension in top-level athletes, muscle stiffness exceeds the stiffness of fascial tissues. This leads to increased elastic recoil in fascial tissues. This could have implications in the validity on strength training with weights for the proper tension and practicing certain types of dynamic Qigong, such as White Tiger Qigong™ for the fascia.

Fatigue is absolutely counterproductive for the fascia. It causes a stretch reflex decrease and a loss of elastic energy potential. I believe this is why my master always impressed upon me to stop before the point of fatigue.

One key to avoiding fatigue is to keep a specific work-rest ratio between sets. For rehabilitation, suggest a ratio of 1:5–1:10. When the exercise takes 10 seconds, 50–100 seconds rest would be appropriate[5].

We rest in our Qigong by doing Zhan Zhuang and concentrating on relaxing the fascia and the whole body. The tempo of your breathing and the movement tempo you choose also determine the effect on your nervous system.

Synchronizing your breathing with the type of Qigong movement necessary for the intended result can attune your nervous system to respond to the conditions of the moment. The nervous system seems to have around six times more sensorial interest in what goes on in the fascial matrix than it does in detecting changes in the muscle itself.

The nervous system plays a crucial role in the improvement of activities. This is known not only from competitive athletes but also from great musicians. What this means is that the frequency of your training and movement patterns facilitate reflex building which finally leads to a most perfect execution of the movement. This is due to the plasticity of the nervous system.

It is vital to remember that movements are always the result of myofascial chains. Every dysfunction of a single member of these chains has a negative effect on the overall movement pattern. So, meridians are not just important for circulation, but crucial for proper movement.

Muscle needs a stable hold in order to make a movement. That is why we need to root properly with each stance firmly pressing into the ground. Think of the body as having been just one muscle that has subsequently subdivided into more than 600 fascial bags. This physical network of your body is made up of a structural material called connec-

[5] Chu & Cordier (2000)

tive tissue. Visceral fascia (also called subserous fascia) suspends the organs within their cavities and wraps them in layers of connective tissue membranes. Each of the organs is covered in a double layer of fascia, these layers are separated by a thin serous membrane. There is a potential space between it and the deep fascia which allows for flexibility and movement of the internal organs.

## Squeezed out Like a Sponge

When putting fascial tissue under strain, fluid is pressed out of the stressed zone, similar to a sponge being squeezed. When releasing the strain, this area will refill with fluid from the surrounding tissue, the lymphatic network and the vascular system.

Even from the Taoist perspective, we see the organs as a sponge and the meridians as a towel; twist the towel to wring it out and squeeze the sponge to eliminate the toxins. White Tiger Qigong has carefully designed Qigong exercises to do just this.

Rhythmically loading and unloading the fascial tissue is an important part of "fascial fitness". This is a core principle in our Qigong.

Nearly 50 percent of a healthy person's lack of range of motion at the joint can be attributed to the tightness of the joint capsule. White Tiger Qigong™ works deeply on opening the range of motion to greater depths at the joint capsules.

The more you do this Qigong, the more your body produces the elements necessary to keep you flexible and strong and to greatly diminish the stiffening effects of age.

When the body does not have good structural alignment (i.e. good posture), it has to endure additional stress and strain in an effort to provide more support as it functions within the pull of gravity. This Qigong is a way to ameliorate injuries from long-term structural imbalances.

## Plasticity and Elasticity

Appropriate counter poses and respect for the elastic limit invite an overall balance to the whole practice. If we go beyond the elastic limit, it is a different state - that of plasticity.

The fabric of connective tissue shows the fascia assisting or resisting your movements. The Neuromusculoskeletal system is wrapped in this amazing material and depends on it to communicate information to and from the brain, spinal cord, and peripheral nerves. The brain and spinal cord is also wrapped in a special connective tissue called dura mater. During Primordial Breathing Qigong, we learn how to contract that connective tissue to stimulate more Qi and circulation to the brain. Actually, your brain is connected to your whole body through this body wide fabric called the fascial network or fascial net. In Qigong, we say the spirit guides the movement. My master always said that the more focused our spirit is during practice, the more sensitive we become to what is happening in our body and outside of it.

Using visualization or feeling in Qigong stimulates chemical releases in the body and neuron signals that produce movement. Through training visualization, you are exercising the messages that travel from the brain and spinal cord through the fascial network and into the muscle to produce movements.

This is why experienced Qigong practitioners can experience incredible feats. They have trained their concentration to a fine point and developed a mind-body connection so that they can more precisely control the signals and amplitude of these signals from the brain to the muscles.

By practicing various motions with a meditative mind, they can sense the meridian connections which are essentially muscle fascia connections. Due to deep movements and the ability to more precisely manipulate their muscle fascia and signals, they can mold their body and control it with extreme precision.

For example, my teacher taught me how to open the pores on my skin at will. It took me a while, but I did it. His instructions were, *"Just use your mind with the breath and a special method of tension."*

Now I am able to perform this with ease. What I cannot do is what my master is able to do with ease, and that is to precisely to control the area of skin he wants to open the pores on. He has gained mastery of these signals in his body. To me, Qigong is about mastering and exploring the amazing potential hidden deep within the body.

The fascia is a highly receptive sensor that sends messages to the central nervous system. It creates responses based on the temperature outside of the body, the body's core temperature and light levels. It is now a well-known scientific fact that lights can affect your sleep even if your eyes are closed and covered. The skin is sensitive to all this.
Based on temperatures inside and outside of the body, the skin can open the pores, close the pores, become more permeable and malleable or tighten and stiffen all without any conscious thought or control.

In our Qigong system, we change the temperature of our body through the Qigong exercises to change the plasticity and elasticity of it through specific movements. Once the desired shapes have taken place and the fascia is open, the desired circulation has been achieved. We then go back to our proper, upright, yet relaxed stance to retrain the nervous system and habituate it to a new and healthier posture.

In this relaxation period of closing the organs, you can completely relax the bones and the fascia and then you are ready to focus and train the spirit to higher levels than otherwise possible. This is the Taoist method of deep relaxation that has been used for thousands of years. This is the point where we can also begin to sense what is really going on in our body on a deeper level when we are more relaxed.

Deep relaxation has immense benefits and it is something that we should do on a weekly, if not daily basis.

Here is a list of things that tension and ongoing stress can cause in the body:

| LIST OF THINGS THAT TENSION AND ONGOING STRESS CAN CAUSE IN THE BODY | | |
|---|---|---|
| Cardiovascular disease | Hypertension | Anxiety |
| Sexual dysfunction | Infertility and irregular cycles | Frequent colds |
| Insomnia and fatigue | Trouble concentrating | Appetite changes |
| Digestive problems | Memory loss | Depression |

In research at Harvard, students who were identified as being easily engrossed in thoughts and images were trained in muscle relaxation and then asked to visualize certain specific images. Relaxation alone increased defenses against upper respiratory infections. The added imagery, however, enhanced the effect. The research was done by Mary Jasnoski, a psychologist, who reported the findings at a recent meeting of the Society of Behavioral Medicine in San Francisco[6].

In looking at our Qigong, even in this one-dimensional perspective, we are using muscle relaxation techniques to relax more deeply.

Here are some of the proven scientific benefits of deep relaxation:

- **Boosts Immunity:** Meditation is known to have a significant positive effect on immune cells and research shows relaxation exercises may boost natural killer cells in the elderly, leading to increased resistance to tumors and viruses.

- **Increases Fertility:** Research suggests women are more likely to conceive when they're relaxed.

- **Improves Heart Health:** Relaxation via meditation (done once or twice daily for three months) significantly lowers blood pressure and psychological distress, and bolsters coping ability in people at increased risk of hypertension.

[6] http://www.nytimes.com/1986/05/13/science/relaxation-surprising-benefits-detected.html?pagewanted=all

- **Improves Mental Health:** People who meditate note reductions in psychological distress, depression, and anxiety.

- **Alleviates Irritable Bowel Syndrome (IBS):** When people with IBS practiced relaxation meditation twice daily, their symptoms (including bloating, belching, diarrhea, and constipation) improved significantly.

## Emotions, Aging and Fascia - the Qigong Solution

After years of negative changes, the fascia will twist, compress, and tighten in some areas while becoming overly lengthened and tense in other areas, negatively affecting the anatomy and physiology of our muscles as well as the rest of our body. As we age, the body's fascia begins to stiffen and lose its elasticity more and more, becoming rigid unless we are regularly opening it through deep movement. For some who haven't even aged, their fascia begins this degenerative process. Possibly, this could be a contributing factor in conditions such as fibromyalgia or in chronic muscle stiffness, as an increased thickness of the endomysium has been shown to characterize fibromyalgia patients.

If you only stretch, your body can become like an over-stretched rubber band. Instability can also arise when excessive stretching or sport-skill training results in hyper-mobility of the joint and muscles of the region but is not balanced with sufficient strengthening. On the flip side, if you only do weight training you will become too rigid and possibly become what some people call "muscle-bound". The White Tiger Qigong™ system is the perfect mesh of strength and flexibility to develop what we call the "bamboo body" - flexible, strong, supple and elastic.

From a fascia perspective, when you practice 5 Animal or 5 Element Qigong, you are expanding the suit you are wearing during each animal movement. You are expanding from the core all the way out to the surface layer of the skin and into the extremities. We have the ability to squeeze and draw in our structure and tissues as a whole, besides being able to stretch and fill or expand them in an omnidirectional way, like with the bladder or the lungs.

We look at the organs like sponges, which absorb toxicity and emotions. Hence, we need to regularly squeeze them out like a sponge. Think about it; you brush your teeth and shower daily (hopefully), but do you also cleanse your insides as well? Organ Qigong does this and more. Each exercise of the 8 Trigram Organ Qigong gently squeezes out the organs like a sponge and then has an expansion phase to allow fresh circulation, which fills the organs with qi. The 8 Trigram Organ Qigong acts as a gentle massage for the organs by moving the spine in almost all possible ranges of motion and movement.

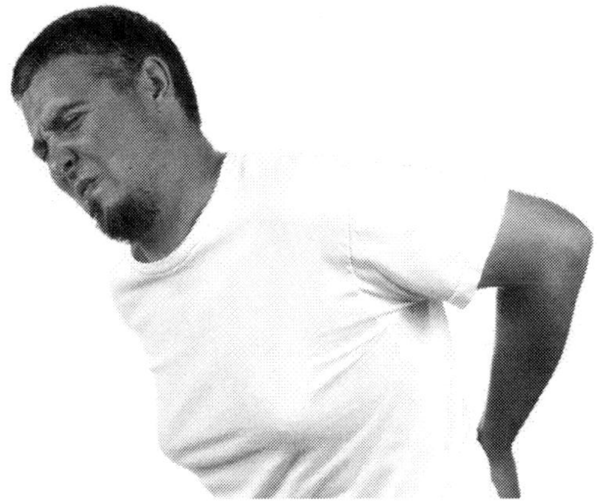

I have worked with some students who had such a weak core, they could not even hold their body up in some basic postures without falling down. Their fascia net was weak and flaccid. Research has shown that before patients can regain functional mobility of their arms and legs, they must reacquire good stabilizing strength in the central, - or core - region of the body. Others have been so tight they cannot move to any depth into the posture. The good news is that both of these problems are solvable through diligent practice. Through dedicated practice, students are able to bring a whole new feeling of strength and suppleness, thereby increasing vitality and an overall sense of well-being.

In my younger years of Qigong, I realized there were many depths to my body. I could actually feel them. After hundreds and thousands of repetitions, I found I could isolate and harmonize different layers and parts of my body. Varying the speed of practice as my master suggested helped me to do this as well.

As I developed my Medical Qigong practice, I discovered how to become keenly aware of the feeling of meridians, organs and even my bones. I could not only sense them, but also coil and uncoil, relax and contract, pumping lots of Qi and promoting deep circulation throughout my body. I discovered how to squeeze out the toxins out of my organs like a sponge on a daily basis. Feeling through the different depths of my body all the way into my bones, it wasn't until I began to desire to learn how to teach Qigong that I discovered what I was actually feeling and doing on an anatomical and fascial level. In my desire to express to people what was happening in Qigong, I began what is now lifelong dedicated research into the modern research of the human body.

As many of you may know by now, not all Qigong is the same. With over 3,000 kinds of Qigong documented today, it is hard to find the right kind of Qigong for you. I was fortunate enough to learn a variety of Qigong techniques from different masters. I kept gravitating towards deep dynamic Qigong because I discovered the benefits of a good balance of static and dynamic Qigong exercises. After trying roughly 40-50 different styles of Qigong, I found actually only about four or five styles that I really wanted to continually practice and explore further because they had depth. These styles, which are now the integral part of White Tiger Qigong's curriculum, seem to have an infinite depth.

The White Tiger Qigong™ system is about fascial restructuring for optimal health, healing and performance. It usually takes three to nine months to see tissue remodeling effects from the outside as well as 'feel' them in palpation. Fascial improvements have a sustainable, cumulative effect and will not be lost quickly (for example, when training is stopped because of health or work-related reasons).

Regular practice of this Qigong for roughly two or three years will definitely be expected to yield long-lasting tissue improvements in the form of an improved strength and elasticity of the global fascial net. Essentially, we seek to preserve and promote elastic integrity.

Movement, first and foremost in this Qigong and many sports, involves a sophisticated interaction of the central and peripheral central nervous system, force-generating muscle and connective tissue, such as fascia, which is intrinsically tied to skeletal muscle. The nervous system seems to be around six times more sensorially interested in what goes on in the fascial matrix than it does in detecting changes in the muscle itself.

Each exercise requires the practitioner to look at a certain spot either in front of the body or at the hands. This is important, as many beginning students start to stare into space or somewhere else that is not relevant to the practice. Any change in eye and head position will have a trickle-down effect on the rest of the body, thus possibly interfering with the actual position and posture of the movement.

Instead of just doing the exercises, you need to go deep within your body, tuning into your entire system. Feel each undulation, stretch, compression and expansion, twist and release, matching each movement with slow breaths to get maximal tissue elongation in broad or specific areas. It is not a state of tension, it is a state of expansion. Trying to explain this in theory is difficult. You must keep practicing this and notice if you have a tendency for tensing too much.

It is important to remember when you perform each movement that you have the movement come from the core of the body out to the extremities. This is the way my teachers all taught me, and interestingly enough this is what fascia research also explains. In the book, "Fascia in Sport and Movement" by Robert Schleip[7]:

> *"...a stretching impulse, aimed at reaching the tendinous tissues, may profit from including some moments in which the lengthened muscle fibers are actively contracting or are temporarily resisting their overall elongation."*
>
> *Robert Schleip, Fascia in Sports and Movement*

In some of the exercises, we are actively contracting our lengthened muscle fibers by pushing into the earth with the feet, while at the same time stretching, such as in the Spiral Palm where you can feel the opposite foot and toes with the hand. For example, as your torso twists to the left, grab the ground with your left foot while your right hand moves with the twist across to the left. Here you will feel the natural tension moving across the body.

[7] Fascia in Sport and Movement by Robert Schleip January 31, 2015

In training Qigong, it takes time and practice to begin to feel the inner depths of movement within the movement. Fascia science tells us that the sensory endings in the skin will be most sensitive to initiated movement. Small movements in the profound tissues allow the big movements closer to the surface. Therefore, to get to the deep tissues inside the body we must first learn how to feel the more external tissues and gradually feel deeper within the body. This coincides with the Qigong theory that the more time you spend practicing in a concentrated manner, the deeper you will be able to feel and sense into the body. With a little practice, you will be able to tell where there is too much give in the tissues and where there is too little, and with a little more practice, you will be able to identify, for example, which layer within the leg is not coordinating with the rest, and apply to those tissues whatever treatment form is at your disposal.

The musculoskeletal system provides form, support, stability, and movement to the body. It is made up of the bones of the skeleton, muscles, cartilage, tendons, joints, and other connective tissue that supports and binds tissues and organs together.

Anatomically, the fascia can be divided into four groups:

**Pannicular fascia:** this is the fascia beneath the skin which covers the whole body except the orifices of the body.

**Axial and appendicular fascia:** this fascial layer represents the fascia of the musculoskeletal system.

**Visceral fascia:** this fascia wraps the organs. It is fixed at the cranial base and throughout the whole spinal column down to the sacrum.

**Meningeal fascia:** This consists of three membranes - the dura mater, arachnoid, and pia mater. These are essentially the membranes that line the skull and vertebral canal and envelope the brain and spinal cord.

During Primordial Breathing Qigong, we are pulsing the brain, which involves bringing a slight tension and relaxation to that area thus stimulating and bringing circulation to the brain. This eventually can be integrated with each movement so the whole body pulses at the same time.

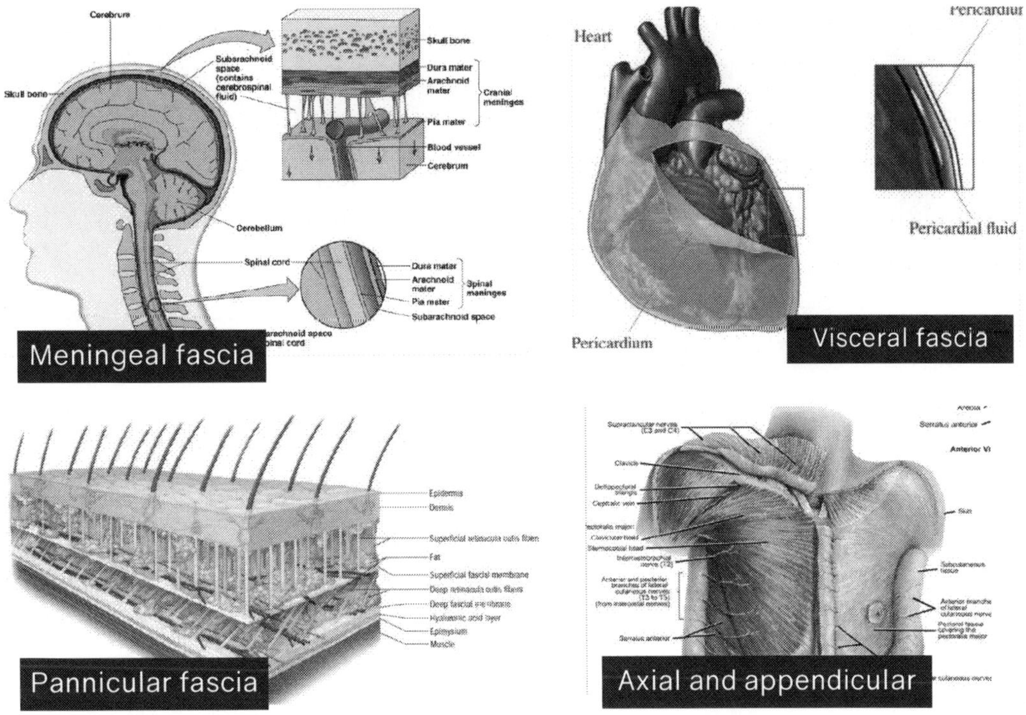


One of the pioneers in research into TCM meridians and fascia is Helene Langevin, a Professor in Neurology from the University of Vermont. Langevin and her team found that most of the Qi points occur where fascia planes or networks converge. They showed that acupuncture points mostly lie along the fascial planes between muscles or between a muscle and tendon or bone. When an acupuncture needle pierces the skin, it penetrates through the dermis and subcutaneous tissue, then through deeper interstitial connective tissue. Langevin hypothesized that a Qi blockage can be viewed as an alteration in the composition of the fascia and that needling or acupressure may bring about cellular change in the fascia[8].

If we take a look at the drawing of "Spiral Qi Lines" by Chen Xin taken from his book, "Illustrated Explanations of Chen Family Taijiquan"[9], what seem like random circular drawings around the body were possibly an early attempt to explain the concept of fascial integrity with what was familiar to Chen at the time - spiral Qi. Another way to look at his drawings are as a rather accurate "force-map" for the major fascial connections in the body. A small excerpt from his book reveals his deep knowledge:

[8] Langevin & Yandow 2002
[9] Illustrated Explanations of Chen Family Taijiquan by Chen Xin

> *"Coiling power is all over the body. Putting it most simply, there is coiling inward and coiling outward, which both appear once one moves. One can feel the coil of the body by turning the feet inwards so you make an upside down V shape with the feet. Then twist from the feet all the way up your spine and even twist into your hands and fingertips. This coiling is easily felt from the big toe all the way into the hands once one becomes proficient in the movement."*
>
> Chen Xin, *Illustrated Explanations of Chen Family Taijiquan*

This is just a prime example of what these practitioners knew about fascia over 100 years ago. One of the masters I studied with most closely always taught me to feel the connection from the toes to my fingertips. When I feel tension on the one foot, to grasp the ground a little more firmly with the toes activates that meridian even more. When I look at this picture, it reminds me of the Spiral Palm (Pan Huan Zhang) in particular. See the 8 Trigram Organ Qigong for that exercise.

五元氣功

# Learning Qigong

## Possible Adverse Reactions to Qigong

### Soreness and fatigue

At the start of practicing Qigong, new practitioners may feel soreness, fatigue, or weakness in the beginning stages. You are doing new exercises, stimulating new energy flows, using new muscles and exercising the body in a new way, which is why it can take some time to adjust. In fact, soreness could actually be a positive result of good Qigong practice. Shooting pain is not good and you should stop the movement if you experience this. Let yourself rest and come back to it once more. If it still persists, stop and seek out the advice of a qualified instructor. If after three days you are still sore from the Qigong, it means you have pushed your body too hard or over- exerted. The next time you practice, do less so that you can recover properly.

### Shortness of breath and difficulty breathing

If you experience shortness of breath during the exercises, it is important to go back to a natural breathing method. Do not try to control or force the breath. A breath that is too shallow or too long can also be a cause of this. In this case, a more balanced, natural breath is advised. Another possibility could be improper posture, and this can be alleviated through proper postural alignments.

## Headaches and dizziness

Concentrating too intensely during Qigong practice can cause headaches. Qigong should always be done gently in a calm and relaxed way. Holding the breath unnecessarily can also cause headaches and dizziness, as the oxygen supply and blood flow will potentially be blocked.

## Menstruation

During menstruation, women are advised to proceed with caution. If the Qigong increases your menstrual flow, cease your practice until your period stops.
Women should not practice Qigong while menstruating heavily as Qigong will likely increase blood flow.

# — Learning Principles

## Learn the components of Qigong then combine them

Learn each movement by itself and then put them together. This is a time-tested Taoist methodology of learning. You must be able to grasp each component to successfully combine it with others.

## Do not fatigue yourself

Get to know your body and how many repetitions it can handle. Stop at the onset of fatigue. Do not let the ego push your body. Knowing when to stop brings forth the ability to conserve proper energy and keep it for the next set or the next day. This is also a principle of the "I-Ching". Once something reaches an extreme, it will turn into its opposite. An example of this is when you train so hard that you become so fatigued that you have no energy left. Always keep a little energy for the next training session.

## Best practices for Qigong

I recommend practicing bare foot on soft, dry grass. This ensures proper stimulation of the acupuncture points on the bottom of the feet. The next best practice is to wear soft, thin-soled shoes that allow your feet to flex and feel the connection to the earth.

**ADDITIONAL TRAINING TIP: Breate Continuously**

*Only hold your breath when instructed by a qualified teacher. Holding your breath while doing certain Qigong can be dangerous as you risk losing your balance, passing out, getting dizzy or simply hurting yourself.*

*Always let your tongue touch the roof of your mouth to connect the Ren and Du Mai (Governing and Conception Vessels).*

五元氣功

# White Tiger Qigong™

## Introduction: Ancient Health and Longevity Wisdom for Modern Society

What differentiates a Qigong master from other practitioners is a high level of concentration, which is the core of the practice of Qigong. Most people lack an ability to concentrate their intention (their Yi), but if you are to heal, transform and reach your potential, you must develop this ability. When you are able to deeply focus and concentrate, you will make things happen and manifest results much more easily with our Qigong practice. Years of sitting in the same posture and going through emotions in those postures has tangled your meridians or your muscle fascia lines. The tissue becomes tight and tangled, while the organs have become compressed. Rather than sitting in their true sphere of comfort, the organs have pressure on them all day long. This is exacerbated by anger, frustration, sadness, or tension.

The same way you need to regularly brush your teeth or take a shower, you also need to wash your insides - opening the meridians, while expanding and contracting the fascia around the organs. Dissected cadavers of people who worked in a seated position over

their lifetimes shows organs displaced into new areas of the body. This pressure on the organs gradually builds more toxins as it becomes more compressed, which then gives rise to emotions they don't understand. They are so focused on their work that they ignored the signals from their bodies.

If you can wake up and brush your teeth, you can wake up and clean your organs by opening your meridians and beginning to oxygenate your whole body. We hardly ever put pressure on the bones when riding in a car or while on a train or sitting all day at work. Through Qigong, we can ward off osteoporosis or muscle and tendon weakness with simple postures to strengthen our bones. You can then restructure your entire body to become more limber, flexible, strong, and resilient.

In White Tiger Qigong™ practice, unlike other Qigong, we are working from the surface all the way into the core of the body. We are strengthening and toning everything in the body. If you are practicing properly, Qigong will have immediate and powerful results.

In this practice, we squeeze out the organs like wringing out a sponge. Toxic energy goes out and pure energy moves in. You're moving the blood while increasing your heart rate and creating greater circulation while moving the lymph around the body. Think of a balloon animal; when you twist one area you inflate, twist, and pressurize. When practicing Qigong, you are moving your muscles and your muscle fascia. After dissecting cadavers, Thomas W. Myers, author of Anatomy Trains, Myofascial Meridians for Manual and Movement Therapists , found that there are lines of muscle fascia (connective tissue) that map directly to the meridian maps in Chinese medicine. When you contract the fascia and expand it, it generates an electrical charge that can be measured with the right instrumentation. Taoist masters teach that to tense and expand, generates Qi internally as this is the yin-yang principle of compression and expansion. One way to think of it is that each day we need to unwind the headphone wires in the body. That is what's happening with the meridians - we get tangled up, unbalanced, tight and in knots. When something is thrown out of balance we may begin to have one side of the body clenched or perhaps an imbalance in the hips, shoulders or the jaw. It can pull your whole being off. If you practice Qigong, the balance in your body will return to normal.

Because the organs and meridians that relate to them are connected to the different emotions in Chinese Medicine, this can result in emotional imbalances. Many people suffer from emotional imbalance and the Chinese see the emotions as connected to the body, the diet, and what you are digesting through all of your senses. If you are taking in stressful information, it will manifest into pain.

Modern fitness programs focus on energizing the muscles through weights, running on a treadmill, increasing the heart rate, and pushing to become stronger. What modern workouts are missing is internal fitness - the fitness of the organs, meridians, bones, fascia, breath, and spirit. It's more complex and takes more time to learn. You can learn how to lift a weight in one minute, but to feel and wring out your spleen may take more time.

Qigong, taught properly, engages the mind, the body, and the breath. It is a complete immersion into total health and well-being, and connects you back together after you get distracted by your external and internal (mental) world.

I have continuously sought out ways to improve my own health, well-being and performance on almost every level. I pay attention to what I eat, the times I sleep and do exercises such as Qigong, Yoga, and meditation. I also pay attention to anything that would hinder or harm my health and performance such as chemicals in soaps, food, etc. Through my tireless pursuits, I have found several styles of Qigong that do just that. They are the most optimal methods of healing, transformation and reaching maximum performance, which is why I relate to people seeking their highest human potential. It does not matter if you are a top athlete looking for the extra edge; the dancer looking for balance and injury treatment and prevention; the yogi looking for something more; the martial artist who wants to add a healing dimension to their practice or even the high-powered businessman who is looking for something to enhance concentration and performance abilities.

As my master told me, you need to keep an open and flexible mind. By finding alternative ways to enhance our existing performance and life we can bring a whole new richness to our life that many will never even discover because they are limited by tunnel vision and disbelief. Believe me, I would not have dedicated my life to these types of practices if I was not reaping huge personal benefits. There is no greater joy than to share with someone overcoming extreme difficulties such as cancer and terrible emotional pain in their own walk of life through this practice. I derive great pleasure in watching some of my students explore the profound depth of their body and existence with Qigong.

五元氣功

# History of White Tiger Qigong™

Throughout Tevia's experiences in seeking out teachers around the world, he realized that most were teaching incomplete forms of Qigong. Most of the types of Qigong he saw taught in the West were extrapolated parts of Tai Chi, isolated and incorrectly called Qigong or Tai Chi Qigong.

Tevia could not understand why anyone would teach this way or why anyone would want to study this way. He realized that most were teaching it this way because most Qigong practitioners only knew Tai Chi as their form of Qigong. It is also important to note that Tai Chi has been heavily promoted and marketed around the world as a form of healing movement. In addition, to learn an entire Tai Chi form can take a long time, while most people in the West don't have this luxury; so, the moves were broken down into easy, fragmented parts that one could learn quickly. This does not do the practice of Qigong justice. Very few people realize that there are over 3,000 kinds of documented Qigong. Tevia was fortunate to have been able to study with various masters since the age of seven. His father had practiced Qigong before Tevia was even born and was able to introduce him to a good master at a young age.

Over the years, he went far beyond what his parents introduced him to and ended up working at a Medical Qigong clinic in China, treating cancer patients. His journey in China led him to study at several Taoist temples, including under unknown hermits and monks.

After four years of very little contact with Westerners, Tevia decided it was time to share his knowledge with people from the West. He observed that most Westerners could not accept the rigorous training style that he personally underwent. He also saw that Westerners placed little faith in what they were told. He realized he would need to prove the efficacy of the Qigong he learned in a Western way. This is when Tevia turned to science and anatomy.

He began to study the Western scientific and anatomical connections of the Qigong he spent a lifetime learning. He found many direct connections and explanations that anyone could understand. Bridging the gap between Western science and ancient Traditional Chinese Medicine has become a passion for Tevia, which has also allowed him to develop his system of White Tiger Qigong™ even further.

Tevia was blessed to be born in an age where he could travel to train with various masters. He also had the background, the ability to speak Mandarin and the understanding of Chinese culture to be readily accepted into secretive Taoist sects. Over 30 years of training led him to create White Tiger Qigong™, a masterpiece Qigong system which is a synthesis of the greatest techniques and teachers in conjunction with modern science and anatomy. He has now become teacher to some of the most well-known Qigong teachers in the world. He has taught best-selling Qigong authors his techniques, and even Taoist Abbots from China have trained with him. All through this, he believes in maintaining a humble approach and deep reverence for his teachers and students alike.

五元氣功

# What *is* White Tiger Qigong™

## Body Mind Spirit

White Tiger Qigong™ is a school of Taoist Qigong, Baguazhang, and Qi Healing Therapies. White Tiger Qigong™ was founded and created by Master Instructor Tevia Feng. The White Tiger School of Qigong's teachings are based on the principles that the body, mind, and spirit must be trained harmoniously as one. In this complete system of training, the student will learn techniques to strengthen the spirit, the body, and the mind through Qigong movement, meditation, and the Taoist internal Martial Art of Baguazhang.

### A Complete Holistic Training Method

White Tiger Qigong™ is a truly unique, fully integrated, holistic system of training of Baguazhang, Xing Yi Quan and Healing Qigong. In ancient times, many traditional Taoist masters were trained in Qigong, martial arts, and healing. Keeping to this ancient tradition, White Tiger Qigong™ offers a truly complete training program. Ultimately, the goal for this system of Internal Arts is health and longevity as it is a physical, mental and spiritual elixir.

### A Unique Qigong Training System

Too often we see teachers teaching only light standing Qigong methods. A complete Qigong training method will involve fully dynamic movements that provide deep stretching and strengthening Qigong exercises. Practices such as Standing Qigong and Sitting Qigong are also key elements, but not the end in themselves as both fit together like a puzzle.

## Flow Like Water, Dance Like Fire

As Master Feng tells his students, White Tiger's principles are that each person contains Yin and Yang, which equates to water and fire. The body must be able to move like a flowing river as fluid as water, but when there is Yang, that needs to be released with fiery explosive Qigong movements.

## Modern Science Meets Traditional Arts

Tevia Feng has sought to bridge modern science with ancient traditional training techniques. White Tiger Qigong offers a uniquely designed training system that teaches the practitioner time-tested, traditional training methods, and principles with modern scientific principles of human anatomy, modern exercise science and muscle fascia research. White Tiger Qigong™ bridges the new and the old world like it's never been done before.

五元氣功

# The Basic Premise *of* White Tiger Qigong™

White Tiger Qigong™ is about healing yourself first and eventually teaching others the self-empowering techniques of self-healing. Once you heal, you go through a transformation that occurs physically, emotionally and spiritually. After this transformation, you'll reach your maximum human potential while maintaining balance and harmony.

五元氣功

# Guiding Principles *of* White Tiger Qigong™

**Healing** is the first and continuous stage of healing old emotional wounds, traumas, and physical abuse that has been inflicted by others or self-inflicted through, amongst others, poor habits and lack of self-care.

**Transformation** occurs after the healing process. We can then go through an alchemy-like process of the body, mind, and spirit realizing total transformation.

**Maximum Human Potential** is each person's ability to realize their innate abilities and refine their limitations, thus realizing their unique and powerful abilities in this human experience. Only after we have healed ourselves and been through the transformation process can we reach this new mountain peak.

**Balance** is the key throughout all the training. Never over fatigue your body or do anything too much or too little.

**Adapting to your environment** means tailoring your Qigong practice to aid you while adjusting to your living environment; whether it is spring, summer, winter, or fall. This also includes your sense of place and weather. Whether it is raining, sunny, dry, or humid, everything is taken into consideration in the way we train Qigong for balance.

## Training balance

- Technical skill to learn the form and technique correctly and properly.
- Physical fitness so that you can perform the Qigong with supple strength.
- Calm spirit so that you can focus on the movements you are doing.
- Proper breathing technique so that you can incorporate the movements with the breath.

五元氣功

# Sports Science and Qigong

This Qigong is used by athletes, martial artists, dancers, ballerinas and yogis who need to train for healing, balance, recovery, flexibility, and strength. When using this Qigong as a supplementary exercise it is important to note that, according to sports science, this Qigong is categorized as:

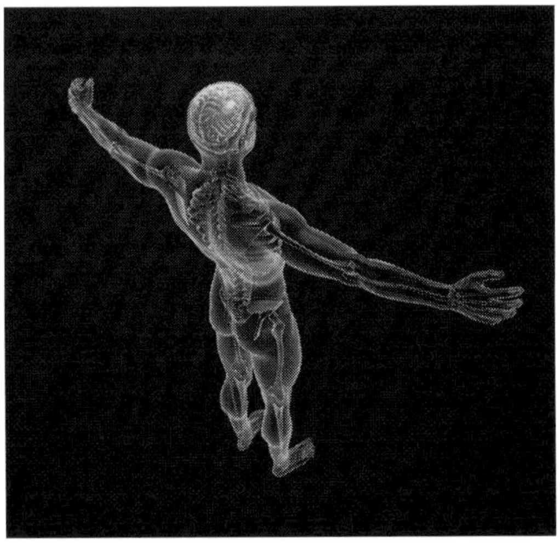

- Dynamic stretching
- Strength and Endurance

White Tiger Qigong's dynamic Qigong exercises from a sports science point of view can be classified as dynamic stretches, strength exercises, endurance exercises, and even endurance strength exercises. Dynamic stretching is best for increasing dynamic or active flexibility which is applicable to everyday life and especially sports.

You can adjust the speed of these exercises to slower or faster tempos. If you are using them as a warm up, I suggest a faster tempo. If you are using them as a method of strength training, I suggest using a slow tempo. In the 5 Element Qigong, you can also sustain a longer hold in the peak phase of each animal form to achieve this aim. From a Chinese perspective, faster is more Yang, while slower is more Yin.

Remember to let the breath direct and guide you as to how long you remain in each exercise. The body responds powerfully to different tempos of breathing. A very slow tempo stretching helps you achieve your most dramatic and permanent gains in flexibility and strength. A faster tempo would be more Yang and a slower tempo would be more Yin. The protocol of a movement (engram) is generated in the motor cortex of the brain. Interestingly enough, in many classic Qigong documents and books, the old wise ones say use your Yi (intention) to tell the body what to do. The Yi is like the General and the Qi is the soldiers.

## White Tiger Qigong™ for Athletic Performance

The White Tiger Qigong™ system is used to enhance performance for, amongst others, athletes, martial artists and dancers. Performance is enhanced by goal-orientated whole movements. Stretching practices which focus internally on specific tissues may actually degrade performance.

The elasticity of large connective structures, such as tendons, changes our thinking about force transmission and efficient movement.

## White Tiger Qigong™ and the Western Anatomical Perspective

From a Western anatomy perspective, these exercises are a type of dynamic stretching that moves the limbs through a greater range of motion than normal.

*"Studies show that static stretches actually have a detrimental effect on explosive movements and strength output. There are two types of flexibility receptors: a static receptor, which measures magnitude and a dynamic receptor, which measures speed and magnitude. Dynamic activities that require movement, such as running, jumping or kicking use the dynamic receptor to limit flexibility. Therefore, a dynamic stretch that stresses the dynamic receptor is more beneficial when preparing for a warm-up when performing a dy-*

*namic activity. Dynamic stretching also includes constant motion throughout the warm-up, which maintains the core body temperature, whereas static stretching cage drop in temperature of several degrees. Another benefit of dynamic stretching is that it prepares the muscles and joints in a more specific manner since the body is going through motions it will likely repeat in the workout. It also helps the nervous system and motor ability since dynamic motions do more to develop those areas than static stretches."*

Following this theory, you could use White Tiger Qigong exercises as a great warm-up or cool-down for another workout, or as a workout in itself. For me and many practitioners, this is our main form of exercise.

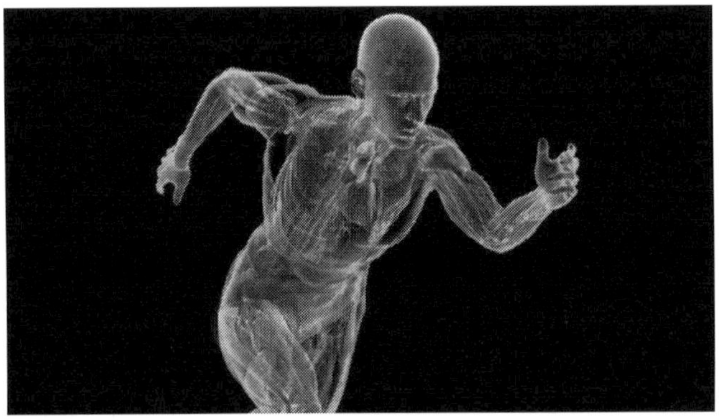

NorCal Strength and Performance (rated one of the top 30 gyms in the USA) explains why dynamic stretching is important to the Meridians. *"Dynamic stretching will be beneficial to your performance and set you up for the current workload! Here is the science. Your body has many mechanisms that need to be activated and stimulated. When you put your body through a series of stretches while in motion, it sends signals from the brain to the muscle fibers and connective tissues in that area to prepare to do work. Your body's temperature begins to rise and blood is pumped to the working areas of the body. Getting good blood flow to the area of the working muscles is very critical in order to supply the area with energy needed to do work. Along with getting proper blood flow to the working area, the muscle fibers and connective tissues will gain more flexibility and range of motion. Many studies have shown that dynamic stretching can help increase power, improve flexibility, and increase your range of motion."*

五元氣功

# Warm-Ups

It is important before you begin your Qigong practice, to properly warm up the body, using a variety of warm-up exercises. The warm-up should last two to ten minutes. Sometimes I do a light jog, jump rope or even just jog in place until I feel my body starting to warm up. If you don't warmup properly, you risk injury as the joints and muscles are cold, thus the fascia is tighter. Below is a great Qigong exercise that I frequently use to warm up. This is also one of the most common Medical Qigong exercises taught in China as it is easy to do, safe and has a very positive effect on your health.

## Letting Go Qigong (Shaking) 5 to 10 minutes

Shake by gently bouncing the body and pushing into the ground. You can also lightly jump off the ground.

It is one of the most common practices taught in Medical Qigong because it is easier to practice than running, especially if you have knee injuries or weak knees. It is a good warm up and it also shakes the organs, which allows them to move more freely in the body, thus it is good to do before Organ Qigong.

After shaking for 5 to 10 minutes, stop and hold a "ball of Qi" between your palms. Begin to breathe in and expand the ball and breathe out as you compress the ball.

Upon completion, allow the palms to settle by your side and practice Ting Jing. This practice makes it easy to feel Skin Qi.

五元氣功

# THE DRAGON

## Water Element - Kidney

*"Symbolizing power, strength, vigor, vitality, wisdom, resilience and growth, the dragon thus reflects positive values, and the values of independence, perseverance and dedication."*

The mythical Chinese Dragon is a symbol of the power of the emperor, of divinity, mysticism, blessedness and benevolence. It is the kind of power only gained outside of the realm of the physical world - like the sun kings of Europe and the deified royalty of the Maya. The emperor was more than human, but possessed of something that transcended this earthly plane.

Dragon myths exist all over the world, from South America to the British Isles, India, Southeast Asia and the great dragons of China. Some breathe fire, others slash with their claws, some have feathers and others are like giant snakes. The kingdom of Bhutan is known in local language as the land of the dragon, and the Bhutanese leaders are called Thunder Dragon Kings. In China, the dragon has closely been associated with the emperors, who took the dragon as their emblem, and the Chinese people are sometimes called "Descendants of the Dragon."

*Relying on the wisdom of the old humaneness, the Tao of the ancient emperors (now practiced by strategic leaders) is put forth; this still has great relevance in an age of rapid changes, and hence its appeal. Positive and harmonious relationships are emphasized, with the country (the world) and its citizens enjoying the 'Big Peace'*[10].

The Dragon form targets our original Jing essence - centered in our kidneys. This is one of the keys to longevity. As we twist to our maximum range of motion through our spine, we wring out the kidneys and stimulate flow in the spine. This builds our capacity to retain this basic life force, given to us by our parents, of which most of us have a finite amount that we use up during our lifetime. The emotion associated with the kidney is fear; this is the place that is most impacted when we are afraid, and in this world of deep fears, as well as constant media bombardment that triggers those base survival instincts, our kidney Jing is in danger of being depleted.

[10]Low, K C Patrick, Applying Strategic Leadership, the Way of the Dragon (January 6, 2010).

I have taught this animal with great success to people with lower back pain and soreness. I worked with martial arts teachers who train in Muay Thai and Krav Maga, who told me this helped open up their lower back and eliminate back pain. One of the common ailments that athletes who train intensively complain about is lower back pain. This is a great solution.[11]

If good kidney function makes an individual feel strong, agile, and energetic, the description of kidney qi deficiency, with lower backache, soft bones, weakness, fatigue, dizziness, and forgetfulness, means it is all just part of the aging process. When we age, or have a decrease in kidney essence, the hair thins and hearing is impaired. The term essence is sometimes used to mean semen. Since aging is the result of a progressive decline in reproductive hormones, it is evident that the TCM view of the kidneys must include the reproductive system.

## Instructions

From the standing meditation posture, open by raising both arms forward to the chest level and then dropping them back down to the waist. From here, turn both hands as if "holding a ball", with the right hand above the left at the level of the navel. Step out with the left foot into a horse stance and then sink the turn into the "bow stance" while the right palm pushes up towards the sky and the left hand moves out laterally to the left as if throwing a frisbee.

[11] Optimal Healing, Patricia Tsang M.D., 2008

Try to turn completely around while keeping both feet planted firmly in a "bow stance." This is the full extent of the motion. Hold this posture for three to nine seconds while comfortably holding a full breath and directing the eyes to the left palm.

From this position, slowly turn back to the front into horse stance, bringing the left foot back so that the feet are again at shoulder width and the arms are parallel to the ground with fingertips facing upwards. In addition to the step, simultaneously circle the arms back to "hold the ball" except this time the right hand is on the bottom. Remember, what is on the outside is also on the inside, so feel the points from your lower Dan Tian to your middle Dan Tian becoming full. Repeat this motion on the right side to complete one whole round; three repetitions on each side make a full set. Once a full set is complete, end the sequence by opening the hands down, out, and up and then closing (see closing chapter for precise instructions). Finish with Zhan Zhuang.

## Check Points

**Stance:**

- Both feet firmly pushing into the ground
- Front foot facing forward
- Back foot turned inward to a 45-degree angle
- Back leg straight and front bent

**Upper Body:**

- Top palm facing the sky over the head
- Back hand facing the sky and at the shoulder level
- Both arms straight
- Maximum twist in the spine

## Anatomical and Physiological Benefits

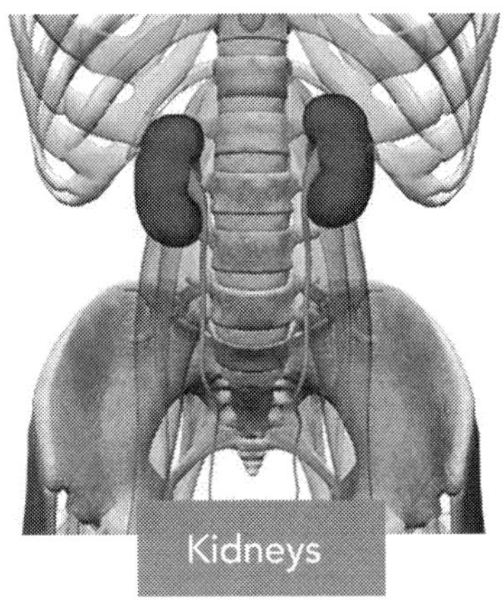


Not only is the twist of the spine good for our kidneys, but the stance Gong Bu (Bow Stance) brings energy to the kidneys as the back leg pushes the force right up into the kidneys. This, combined with the deep twist, gives a good squeeze of the kidneys from the bottom up and a twist squeezing them at several angles (see figure for the placement of the kidneys). As you sink deep into the stance, you can feel it stimulating your lower back and kidneys. Do not slack, and make sure to sink deep into this stance to reap maximum benefit.

## Effects on the Fascia

As you can see in figure, to engage the kidney meridian you need to firmly plant your back foot into the ground. If the foot is turned out too far you won't get the proper tension needed on the kidney meridian. The twist in the Dragon wrings out the meridian as it travels up your centerline of the body. The arm positions aid in a further opening of the kidney meridian as well as the psoas. It is important to look at your hand or beyond that to engage the Spiral Line all the way up into your neck.

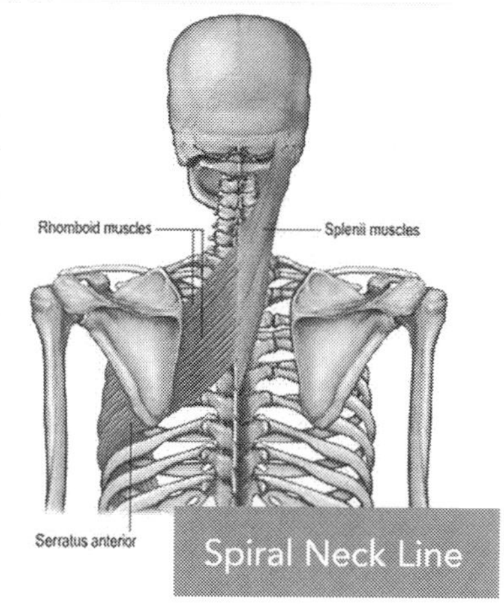

Spiral Neck Line

The lifting of the arm on the side of the body being stretched adds more stretch to the Spiral Line while the lower arm is going in the direction of the contracted part of the Spiral Line, thus acting to increase the contraction. By engaging the Dragon deep into the deep fascia, you will engage the Deep Front Line through the psoas.

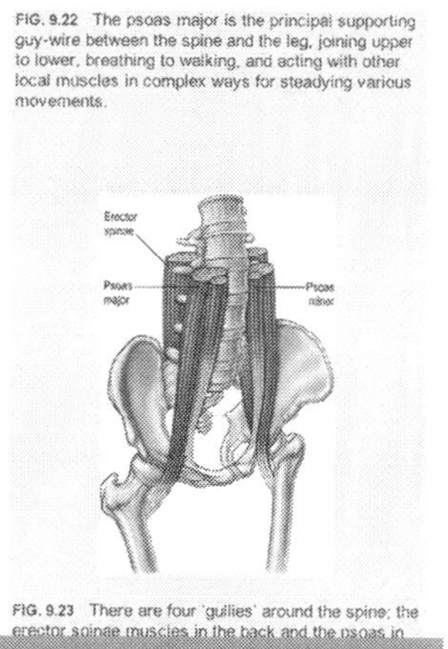

Deep Front Line Psoas

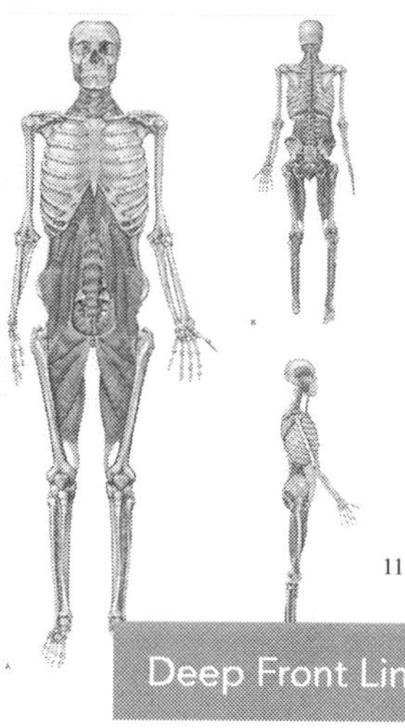

Deep Front Line

[12] Reprinted from Anatomy Trains: Myofascial Meridians for Manual and Movement Therapists, 3E, Thomas Meyers, 2014, with permission from Elsevier

The deep twisting engages the Spiral Line.

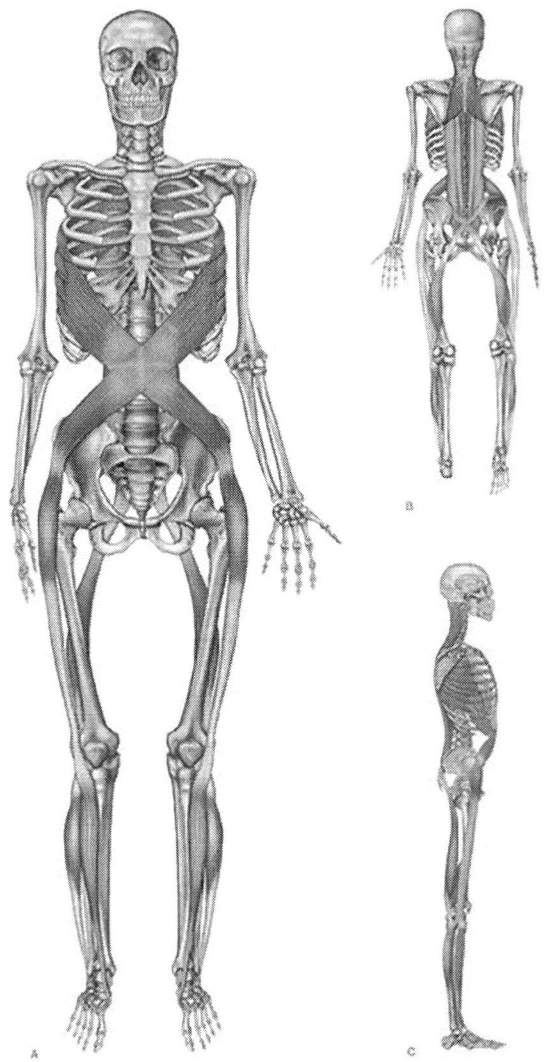


[12]

## Effects on the Meridians

The kidney and bladder meridians are engaged by having the foot at a 45-degree angle, turned inwards with the leg straightened. As you twist you can feel "lines" from your feet going up the legs and into the torso twisting. To distinguish this try turning the foot out to a 90-degree angle and twist. You will not feel the twist of the "lines" in the legs. I have my students do this often to show them how to more precisely feel the meridians.

[13] Reprinted from Anatomy Trains: Myofascial Meridians for Manual and Movement Therapists, 3E, Thomas Meyers, 2014, with permission from Elsevier

# — About the Meridians

## The Kidney Meridian - Root of Life, Reservoir of Energy, and Seat of Courage & Willpower

### Function and Qualities

The kidney meridian is a yin meridian (flows upwards), paired with the bladder meridian. It controls the growth and development of bones and nourishes the marrow, which is the body's source of red and white blood cells.

A weak kidney is therefore a prime cause of anemia and immune deficiency.

In traditional Chinese medicine, the spinal cord and the brain are forms of marrow, and therefore poor memory, inability to think clearly, and backache are all regarded as indicators of impaired kidney function and deficient kidney energy.

The kidney meridian's vitality is reflected externally by the condition of head and body hair and is associated with the entrance hole of the ears. Tinnitus (ringing ears) is thus a sign of kidney dysfunction[14].

The kidneys are also the seat of courage and willpower, and therefore any impairment in the kidney meridian results in feelings of fear and paranoia, and can have an impact on the bladder. The kidneys are responsible for filtering waste metabolites from the blood and moving them onwards to the bladder for excretion in urine. As such, intense fear can cause involuntary urination, a phenomenon also known to Western medicine.

Along with the large intestine, the kidneys control the balance of fluids in the body.

**Element:** water

[14] http://www.shen-nong.com/eng/principles/kidneymeridian.html

**Physical Imbalances:** chest pain, asthma, abdominal pain, irregular menstruation, impotence, hernia

**Emotional Imbalances:** hysteria, paranoia, depression, fear, loneliness and insecurity

**When Balanced:** wisdom, rationality, clear perception, gentleness and self-understanding

**Peak Hours:** 5-7pm

### Route

The Kidney Meridian starts from the inferior side of the small toe. Crossing the middle of the sole and the arch of the foot, it circles behind the inner ankle and travels along the innermost side of the lower leg and thigh, until it enters the body near the base of the backbone. After connecting with the kidney, it comes out at the pubic bone. Over the abdomen, it runs externally upwards until it reaches the upper part of the chest (the inner side of clavicle). A second branch emerges from the kidney and moves internally upwards and passes through the liver, diaphragm, lungs and throat, finally terminating at the root of the tongue. Another small branch divides from the lung to connect with the heart and the pericardium.

## The Bladder Meridian – Guardian of Peace

### Function and Qualities

The bladder meridian is a yang meridian and is paired with the yin kidney meridian. This meridian is the longest and most complex meridian.

**Element:** water

**Physical Imbalances:** headaches, back problems, urinary problems including excessive urination and incontinence, pain in the eyes, tearing and colds.

**Emotional Imbalances:** lack of energy, being inflexible and fearful. Resisting change and basic negative attitude are also expressions of bladder meridian imbalance.

**When Balanced:** Hopeful, looking forward, calm and peaceful

**Peak Hours:** 3-5pm

## Route

It starts at the inner portion of the eyelid and travels across the front of the head to the back of the head. It then forms two branches that travel down the back to the sacrum along the spine. It then goes along the middle of the butt, and then to the back of the thigh. The two branches then meet behind the knee and travel between the calf along the Achilles tendon to the outside of the foot. The Bladder Meridian ends at the outside of the baby toe.

五元氣功

# THE TIGER

## Metal Element - Lungs

*"The spirit of the White Tiger combines the courage and fierceness of a soldier with an ethereal, magisterial dignity. In ancient times, the head of the White Tiger graced the shields of soldiers going into battle, the entrances to important fortifications and the bows of the Emperor's fastest ships.[15]"*

The path you are embarking upon is the path of the White Tiger - the king, the metal element forged in the earth, and the power of physical, mental, and emotional strength. The tiger is powerful and strong, and in China is referred to as the King of Beasts. The tiger is associated with military might and power; a general might be referred to as a tiger. The symbol on the forehead of the white tiger means king.

The white tiger, for whom this Qigong is named, is the highest of the animals in the Chinese pantheon. It has mystical significance and abilities and as the king of the animals, the white tiger possesses incredible power. It was said that the white tiger would only appear when the emperor ruled with absolute virtue, or if there was peace throughout the world. Ancient astronomers in China named the twenty-eight stars near the ecliptic "the twenty-eight mansions". The mansions of the west were collectively named the White Tiger.

In nature, the tiger is the largest member of the cat family in Asia, weighing up to 660 lbs. They like water and are good swimmers, climbers, and runners. A tiger's roar is so loud it can be heard two miles away, yet a tiger can be so quiet that it can get close enough to its prey to pounce.

Fossil records show that tigers in China may be 2 million years old.[16] However, now these magnificent animals are critically endangered, as both climate change and human encroachment into their territories has decimated their populations; poaching is also an enormous threat. At the time of this writing, there are only 3,200 tigers left in the wild.

[15] http://www.crystalinks.com/satoko.html
[16] http://www.worldwildlife.org/species/tiger

The Tiger form opens the lungs, releases grief and stress, and allows us to expand our capacity to breathe. It begins with the expansion of the chest and with retracting our "tiger claws", then pushing them out and expelling all our air. Poor lung function can impair oxygenation of blood, and therefore the skin and hair, suffering this loss, can become dry. We know, for example, that smoking (which obviously affects lung performance) is associated with premature aging of skin. Some TCM treatments, in fact, address skin diseases by treating the lungs.[17] The Tiger form may also be utilized to promote greater lung health and ameliorate associated problems.

In terms of emotional release, when someone is grieving, they 'close up', often times slumping forward, thus restricting movement and the full expansion of the lungs. We can counteract this with the movements of the Tiger, which deeply open the lungs.

## Instructions

From the standing meditation posture, open the same way as in the Dragon by letting the arms rise and fall in front in time with the breath. From here, step out with the left foot to assume a standard "horse stance."

Again, bring the arms up the front with an inhale, but this time draw the hands back so that they are near the shoulders.

[17] Optimal Healing, Patricia Tsang M.D., 2008

Now, with the exhale, sink deep into the "horse stance" and tuck in the tailbone while pressing both palms forward; the fingers should be bent at the tips so as to resemble a "tiger paw."

With the inhale, circle both hands outward and then draw them back towards the shoulders. Turn the palms towards you, facing inwards to stimulate the lung meridian. Then, with the exhale, push the arms straight back with the hands still in a "tiger paw" to stretch the chest and shoulders, extending the wrists behind you.

It is important to feel the twist from the lung point all the way in the upper chest to the hand and thumb to get the lung meridian. With the inhale, turn the hands again, and relax as the hands are drawn forwards and then back to the shoulders in a scooping motion. This completes one whole round; three rounds make a full set.

Once a full set is complete, close by pushing the hands forward and bringing the left foot back so that the feet are again at shoulder width. Allow the hands to drop back to the waist and assume the standing meditation posture; enjoy the standing Qigong for another three minutes.

## Check Points

**Stance:**

- Wide and low horse stance

**Upper Body:**

- Chest arched to the max by pulling the shoulder blades together
- Arms rotated inwards to the max
- Back straight

## Anatomical and Physiological Benefits

By pulling the arms back with the elbows up, you really give a good stretch to the chest, deeply opening the lungs. As you press forward and curl the tail bone underneath you compress the lungs and the digestive organs together, completely expelling and squeezing out the lungs.

During the inhalation phase of the Tiger, you can see the muscles that you are engaging. Notice the pectoralis muscles (chest muscles) are engaged, which helps open the lungs deeper. Thus, the Tiger utilizes these muscles in opening and closing the chest.

During the exhalation phase of the tiger, a forced exhalation is created by engaging the internal intercostal, transversus thoracis and abdominal muscles. Make sure to contract the abdominal muscles here to get the maximum exhalation. This will also serve to tone the abs.

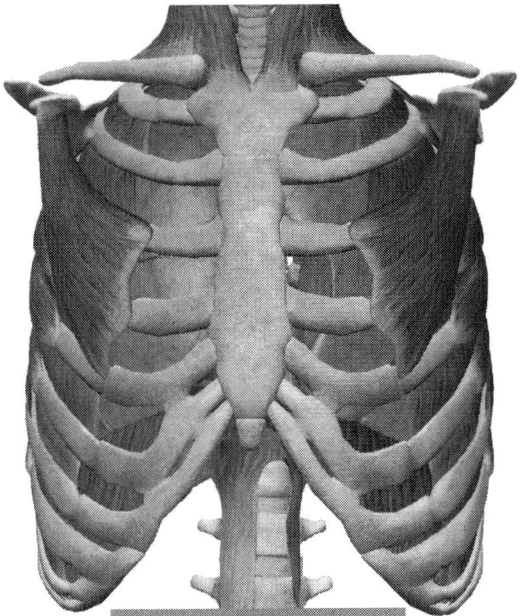

Muscles of Inhalation

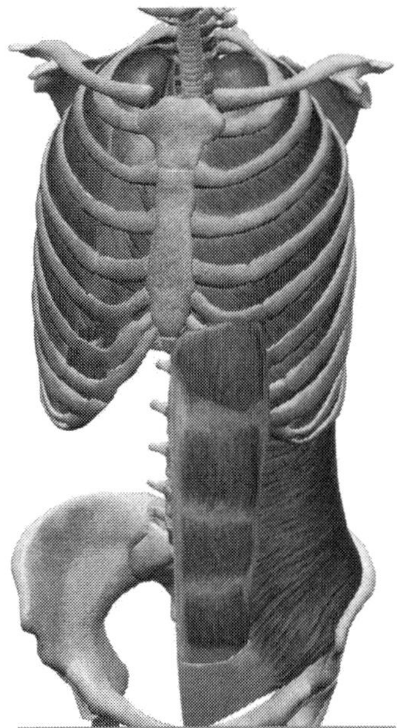

Muscles of Exhalation

## Effects on the Fascia

The Tiger engages the Arm Lines through the deep twisting combined with the pushing forward and pulling backwards. This has many benefits to people with tight shoulders and chests. I have used this successfully with surfers and weight lifters, who suffer from tightness in these areas. People who work at desks a lot will also greatly benefit from the Tiger as they are in a chest- contracted position throughout the day.

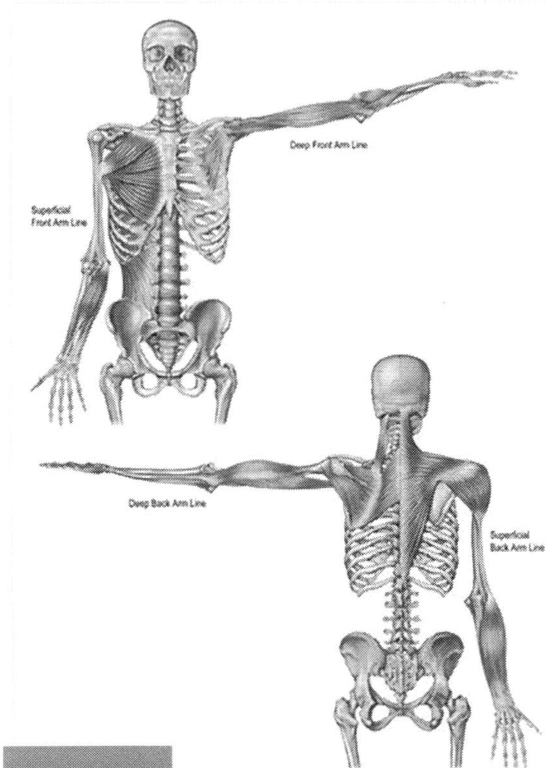


Arm Lines[18]

[18] Reprinted from Anatomy Trains: Myofascial Meridians for Manual and Movement Therapists, 3E, Thomas Meyers, 2014, with permission from Elsevier

## Effects on the Meridians

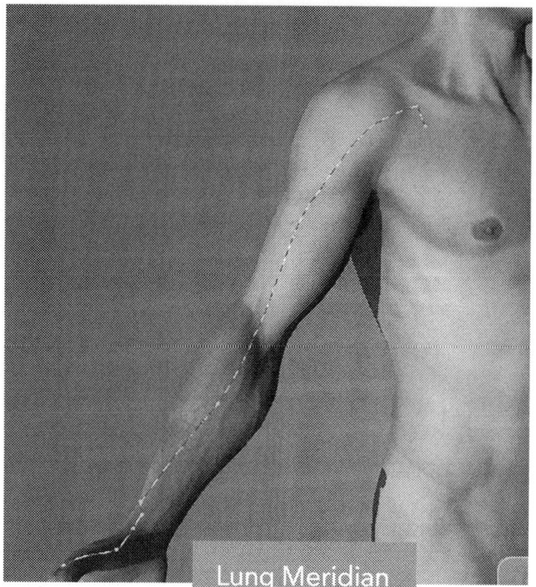


The lung meridian (pic of lung meridian here) is engaged through the deep twisting combined with the pushing and pulling of the arms in Tiger. To truly engage the lung meridian, make sure to get a deep twist all the way from your hands to the shoulder. Do it slowly and gently, to feel deeper into the tissue and meridian. This wrings out the meridian. Feel it combined with the stretch of each push and pull, and experience deep lung meridian opening.

# — About the Meridians

## The Lung Meridian – Controller of Breath and Energy

### Function and Qualities

The lung meridian is a yin meridian which controls breath and energy and it is paired with the large intestine meridian. Together with the heart meridian, it assists with circulation of the blood. Breathing also directly controls the autonomic nervous system, which is why it is the basis for meditation and qi exercises (Qigong, Yoga, and other modalities). Breathing hence forms a bridge between body and mind.

**Element:** metal

**Physical Imbalances:** disorders of the chest, lung, throat and nose

**Emotional Imbalances:** The Lungs are responsible for establishing the foundation of Qi for the entire body. The Lungs house the body's 'Seven Emotions' and are responsible for self-protection and self-preservation. Their negative attributes are disappointment, sadness, grief, despair, anxiety, shame and sorrow.

**When Balanced:** righteousness, dignity, integrity and high self-esteem

**Peak Hours:** 3-5am

### Route

This meridian begins deep in the solar plexus region (middle burner) and descends to meet the intestine. Winding up past the stomach, it crosses the diaphragm, divides, and enters the lungs. It then re-unites, passes up the middle of the windpipe to the throat and divides again, surfacing in the hollow region near the front of the shoulder (LU-1). From here it passes over the shoulder and down the front of the arm along the outer border of the biceps muscle. It continues down the forearm to the wrist just above the base of the thumb (LU-9). The channel crosses the height of the thumb muscle to finish at the corner of the thumbnail.

## The Large Intestine Meridian - Minister of Transportation

### Function and Qualities:

The large intestine meridian is a yang meridian and is paired with the lung meridian.
It controls the transformation of digestive wastes from liquid to solid state and transports the solids outwards for excretion through the rectum.

It plays a major role in the balance and purity of bodily fluids and assists the lungs in controlling the skin's pores and perspiration.

**Element:** metal

**Physical Imbalances:** Paired with the lungs, the large intestine depends on the lungs for movement via the expansion and contraction of the diaphragm, which works like a pump to give impetus to peristalsis by regulating abdominal pressure.

Sluggish bowels may be stimulated by deep diaphragmic breathing and by tonifying lung energy. Congested lungs and clogged bronchial passages may be cleared by purging the bowels.

Symptoms include abdominal pain, intestinal cramping, diarrhea, constipation and dysentery as well as disorders of the mouth, teeth, nose and throat.

**Emotional Imbalances:** The large intestine meridian is affected by the emotions of sadness, grief and worry.

An energetic imbalance in the large intestine can result in physical weakness and provoke emotional introversion, accompanied by feelings of depression, irritability, discouragement, distress and apathy and low self-esteem.

**When Balanced:** righteousness, dignity, integrity and high self-esteem, which is the same as for lungs

**Peak Hours:** 5-7am

## Route

This meridian begins by the outside corner of the index fingernail. It runs along the edge of the finger, between the two tendons of the thumb at the wrist joint and along the outer edge of the arm to the elbow. It continues to the outside of the shoulder muscle, then crosses the shoulder blade and travels upward over the muscle at the side of the neck to the cheek, passing through the lower gums, then over the top lip. The large intestine meridian ends beside the nostril.

五元氣功

# THE LEOPARD

## Wood Element - Liver

*"If we want things to stay as they are, things will have to change.[19]"*

How do you cope with anger and frustration? Are you able to let go and surrender to what is happening in the moment? Do you hold on to the past, letting frustrations and resentment eat away at you, or can you stay focused in the present moment, unaffected by past traumas and dramas?

In the Peruvian Amazon shamanic tradition, the jaguar, a close relative to the leopard, is said to represent "stalking that which is stalking us". This is a perfect metaphor for the practice of the leopard form - targeting the liver, the organ that is associated with anger and toxicity, that must purify our bodies so that we are not consumed by those things that might kill us.

*"If liver Qi [function] is congested, a person will anger easily, have chest and flank swelling and pain, and women will have irregular periods. If liver Yang [force] is rising upward, one will have headache and dizziness. If more severe, the eyes will ache, get red, and if even more severe, a stroke could ensue. Liver is closely linked with emotions. If liver Qi is deficient, the patient is easily frightened or angry." -Optimal Healing by Patricia Tsang M.D.*[20]

The liver filters and detoxifies the blood, produces hundreds of enzymes and hormones, and regulates the volume of circulating blood. Oftentimes, due to poor diet, stress, irritability, and inactivity, the Liver becomes clogged and sluggish. For this vital organ to work properly, it must become decongested and supple.

The Leopard form targets the liver, squeezing the organs as we push the sides of the body together and twist. The liver is the organ of detoxification and purification. It processes impurities in the body, protecting us from them so they do not kill us.

[19] The Leopard, Giuseppe Tomasi di Lampedusa, 1958
[20] Qigong Through The Seasons – Spring, Ronald H. Davis, 2015

## Instructions:

From the standing meditation posture, open in the same manner as in the previous movements and circle the hands to "hold the ball" with the left hand on the bottom. Step out with the left foot into a "bow stance" and let the right hand remain stationary as the left hand moves out laterally to the left side as if throwing a frisbee.

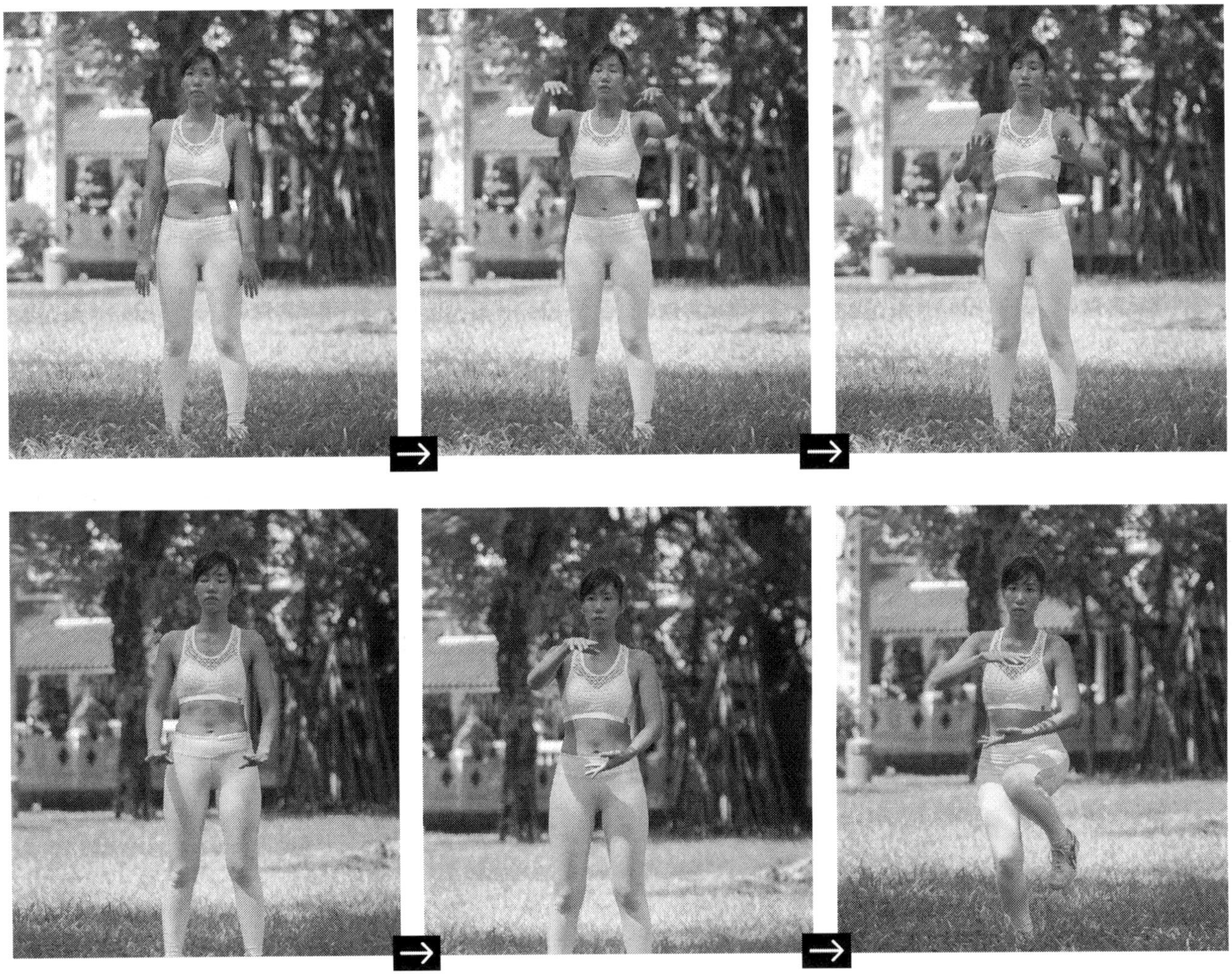

Once fully extended to the left, turn back and sink into a "horse stance" with the feet and knees turned out to a 45-degree angle, which opens the liver meridian. Keep the weight balanced 50/50 on both legs as much as possible and press the big toe into the earth to further activate the liver meridian. At the same time, the left hand pushes back, behind the neck and over to the right side; in time with this movement, allow the right palm to face up as if to protect the left armpit.

This is the full extent of the motion; try to hold it comfortably with a full breath for at least three to nine seconds while the eyes are wide open remaining fixed on the extended left hand.

From here, allow the left hand to drop down as the body returns to a "horse stance." In a continuous motion, bring the left foot back to shoulder width and circle both hands back to "hold the ball", with the right hand now on the bottom. Repeat this motion on the other side to complete one round; three rounds make a full set. After a full set, close in the same way as in the Dragon by opening the hands down, out, and up as if outlining a huge ball. Gather the energy, bringing it over the head and down through the body until you reach the lower Dan Tian. Once again assume the Zhan Zhuang Standing Qigong posture. Stay in this meditation for at least 3 minutes.

## Check Points

**Stance:**

- Feet turned out to a 45-degree angle minimum
- Weight even on both feet
- Knees both bent

**Upper Body:**

- One palm facing out, covering armpit area
- Top palm fingers stretched back, aiming behind you
- Arm straight and stretching over your head and behind you

## Anatomical and Physiological Benefits

By bending deep to the right, you compress the liver. By extending your arm, you will get an even deeper compression. With an added slight twist in your spine, your right shoulder comes forward so you will get an even deeper twist and compression of the liver, thus squeezing it out deeply.

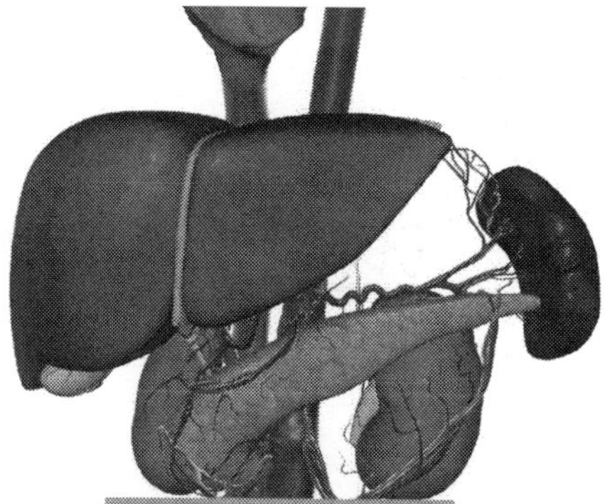

Liver and Spleen

## Effects on the Fascia

The Lateral Line (LL) is involved with stability. Specifically, it is used in keeping the body stable with side to side movements. By bending sideways, you activate the LL. The fascia that moves up the spine is engaged in a contraction and stretching phase as well.

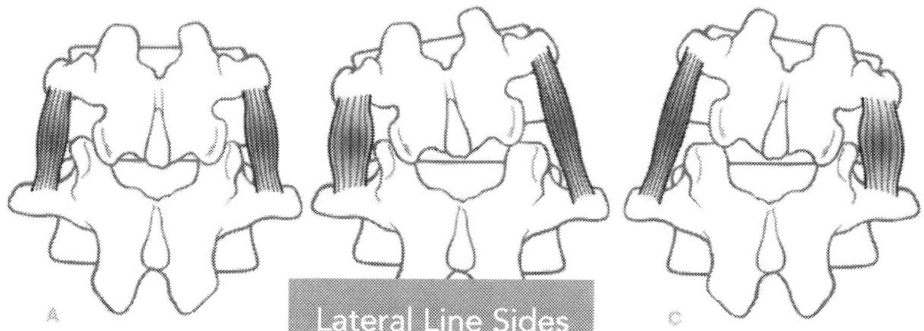

Lateral Line Sides

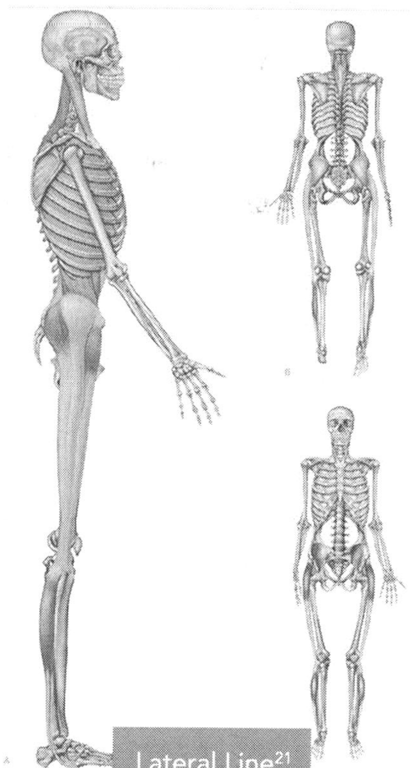

Lateral Line[21]

The LL is almost identical to the gallbladder meridian, which is interesting because the gallbladder meridian is the opposing meridian to the liver. (see below in the meridian pictures).

[21] Reprinted from Anatomy Trains: Myofascial Meridians for Manual and Movement Therapists, 3E, Thomas Meyers, 2014, with permission from Elsevier

Try to feel the LL up into the neck as you twist your spine in the peak of the movement; feel your neck also gently twisting too.

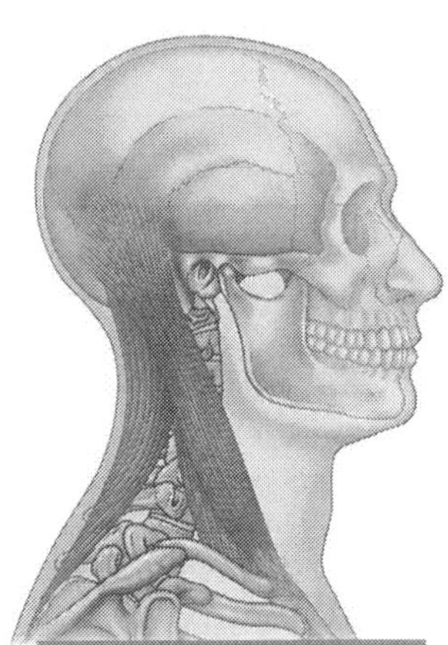

Lateral Line Neck

The LL brackets each side of the body from the medial and lateral mid-point of the foot around the outside of the ankle and up the lateral aspect of the leg and thigh, passing along the trunk in a 'basket weave' or crossed-shoelace pattern under the shoulder to the skull in the region of the ear.

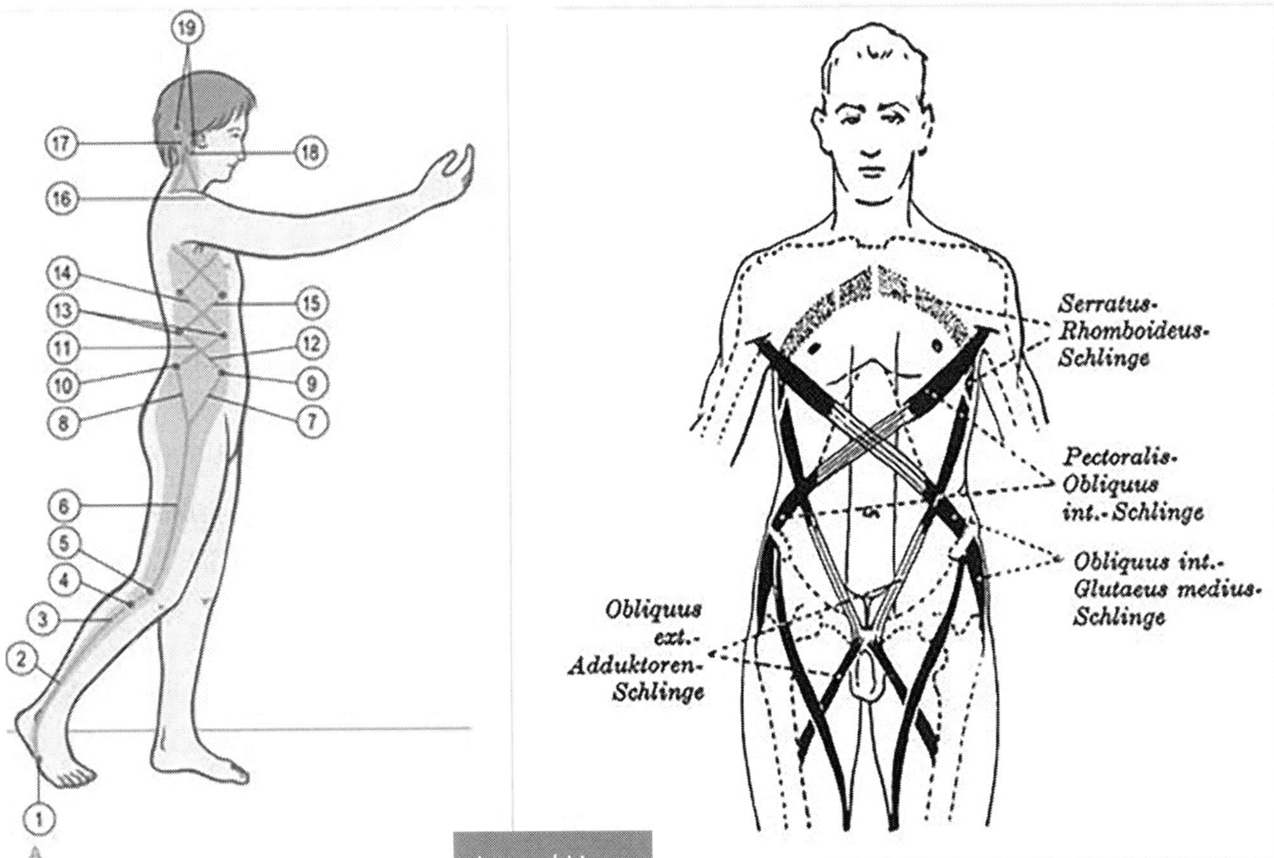


Lateral Line

The LL functions posturally to balance front and back, and bilaterally to balance left and right. The LL also mediates forces among the other superficial lines – the Superficial Front Line, the Superficial Back Line, all the Arm Lines, and the Spiral Line. The LL often acts to stabilize the trunk and legs in a coordinated manner to prevent buckling of the structure during activity.

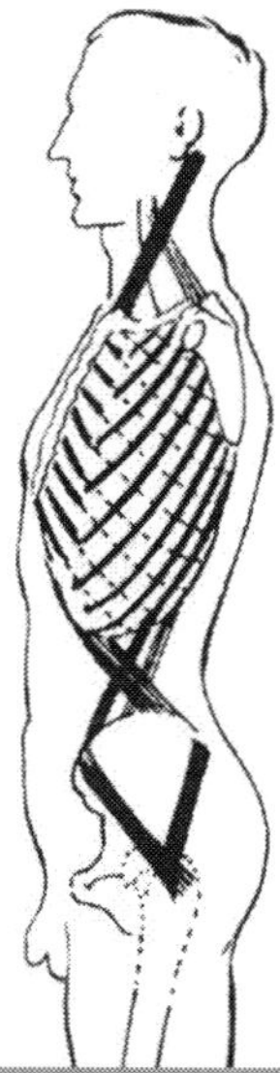
X Lateral Line

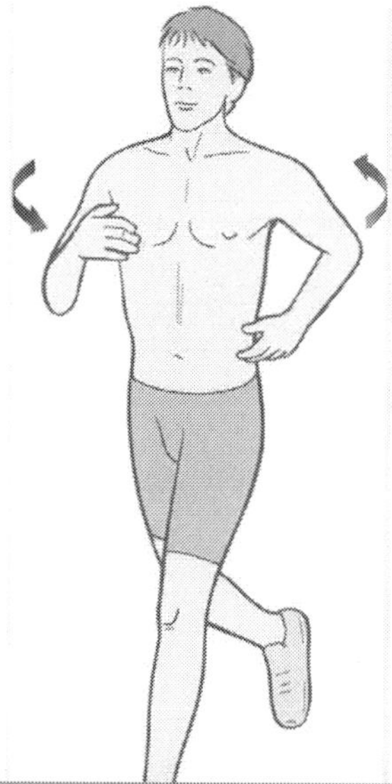
Lateral Line Jogging

The LL can be seen in action in jogging, as the rib cage winds and unwinds with each step. You can also really feel this LL engagement in the Leopard, with the deep twist at the peak of the movement.

## Effects on the Meridians

By opening the groin, legs and feet outwards, we activate the liver meridian.

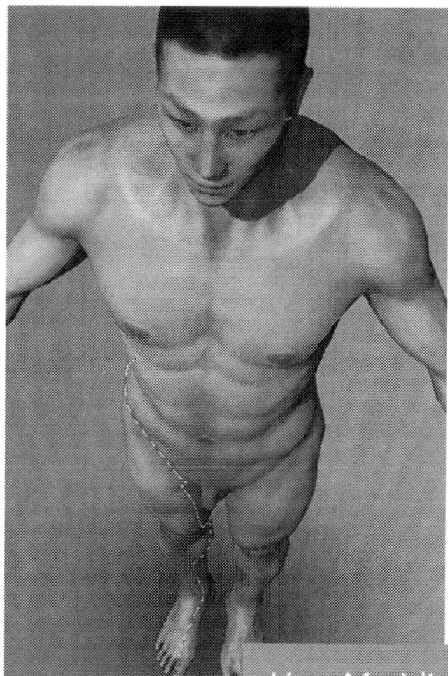
Liver Meridian

# About the Meridians

## The Liver Meridian – Replenisher of Blood

### Function & Qualities

The Liver Meridian is a yin meridian paired with the Gallbladder Meridian. . It is responsible for filtering, detoxifying, nourishing, replenishing, and storing blood. It regulates the amount of blood circulating, withdrawing and storing it when resting or sleeping, and releasing it during exercise.

**Element:** wood

**Physical Imbalances:** Liver function is reflected externally in the condition of finger- and toenails and by the eyes and vision. Blurry vision is often a result of liver malfunction rather than an eye problem.

**Emotional Imbalances:** The liver governs growth and development, drive and desires, ambitions and creativity.

Obstruction of liver energy can cause intense feelings of frustration, rage, and anger, as well as irritability, resentment, jealousy and depression.

**When Balanced:** kindness, compassion, and generosity

**Peak Hours:** 1-3am

### Route

The Liver Meridian starts inside of the big toenail, crosses the top of the foot, passes in front of the inside ankle and up the inner aspect of the leg. It continues upwards, passes the knee, and continues along the inner thigh to the groin and pubic region, where it circulates to the external genitals. It connects with the conception vessel in the lower abdomen and further up enters both the liver and gallbladder. The meridian then dips into the rib cage, runs up through the throat, opening to the eye, and ends at the crown of the head where it connects with the governing vessel.

## The Gallbladder Meridian - for Courage and Initiative

### Function & Qualities

The Gallbladder Meridian is a yang meridian and is paired with the liver meridian. This Meridian's Qi (energy flow) is responsible for decision making and good judgments, among other things, as well as providing courage and initiative.

**Element:** wood

**Physical Imbalances:** insomnia - waking up suddenly very early in the morning and not being able to fall asleep again, tendons, tears, nails, eye diseases, glaucoma, and night blindness, stiff neck, ringing in the ears, dizziness

**Emotional Imbalances:** timidity, indecision, being easily discouraged, resentment

**When Balanced:** courage and initiative, decision making and good judgment, sound sleep, healthy expression and processes of creativity, planning, brainstorming, analysis, and decision-making

**Peak Hours:** 11pm-1am

### Route

This meridian begins just outside the outer corner of the eye, turns down towards the ear and then up to the forehead just within the hair line, then descends behind the ear to the corner of the skull. It then returns to the forehead above the center of the eye and moves down the head to the bottom of the skull. It continues down the neck to the shoulder, descends the side of the body along the ribs, to the waist and pelvis. It continues down the outside of the leg, to the ankle, ending on the outside of the 4th toe.

五元氣功

# THE SNAKE

## Earth Element - Spleen

*"The soft and pliable overcomes the hard and inflexible.*
*Just as fish remain hidden in deep waters,*
*it is best to keep weapons out of sight."*

The snake slithers stealthily through the grass, and strikes fast. The snake also sheds its skin and is completely remade and reborn, all at once. Unlike the other animals in this set, the snake is not endangered; the snake is ancient and lives on - adapting to all environments. Snakes live all over the world, on every continent except Antarctica. It seems a deep primal response to fear the snake, as the snake can sneak up on us and move so quickly we have no hope of escaping its deadly bite or squeeze.

The snake works on the spleen - an organ that in Chinese Medicine is related to the digestion of food Qi - getting nutrition from food and good digestion. The spleen has a tendency to get too damp, and when the spleen is damp mucus can form, digestion goes off, and we can experience anxiety or worry. To reduce dampness, TCM herbal prescriptions often times act as a diuretic. Through compression and "squeezing" out of the spleen we can increase the diuretic function. The Spleen: "The spleen governs blood. It makes blood and regulates the circulation and direction of blood flow. If there is malfunction, the symptom is deficient-type bleeding. The Spleen governs muscle. This governance goes all the way to the mouth and flourishes in the lips. If the Spleen is in good condition, the person is muscular and lips are red. If the Spleen is in poor condition, there is decreased muscle tone, and lips are withered and colorless."[22]

Rumination, or worrying something over and over, is associated with the spleen. Stagnant Qi is also related to the spleen. Symptoms like phlegm arise from issues with the spleen. The spleen creates stagnation easily.

The Snake form opens with the snake slithering up the body, looking back, creeping through the grass, and returning to the center of the body. The 'creeping through the grass' movement compresses the organs, squeezing them out like a sponge. The organs are further expanded as the torso returns to the center of the body, and thus absorb fresh energy.

[22] Tao Te Ching, Lao Tzu

## Instructions

From the standing meditation posture, open again in the same way as for the other forms. After the opening, draw the left hand back and the right hand forward as if outlining two circles. While stepping the right foot out into a "bow stance", bring the left hand over to the right side as the right hand slides laterally- palm up - up the left arm, moving over and beyond the left palm.

From here, turn the right hand over so that it is now palm down and move the left hand down as the body sinks into a "snake creeps through grass" posture.

While remaining low, shift the weight to the left side and lead with the left hand as the entire body leans over to the left side. From here, move the right hand behind the head, and over to the left side over the left hand, holding a qi ball. This is the full extent of the posture. Hold the ball with a full breath for at least three to nine seconds while keeping the eyes focused on the right hand.

From this posture, simply drop the right hand so that the body is now in position to repeat the same movement on the other side. Completing the motion once on both sides makes one round; three rounds complete a full set. After a full set, the closing movements are made by standing back up and moving the right leg back to a shoulder width position while the arms gather and close in the same manner as the dragon and leopard movements. End with the hands over the Dan Tian and enjoy the Zhan Zhuang for at least three minutes.

## Check Points

**Stance:**

- Front foot facing directly forward
- Back foot turned inwards
- Back leg straight

**Upper Body:**

- Both hands reaching to the max
- Both palms facing pointing in the same direction
- Stretching the body in the direction of your hands

## Anatomical and Physiological Benefits

During the contraction phase as you go into the "creeping through the grass" phase of the movement, you will pay attention to squeezing out the spleen on the left side. This also squeezes out the small intestines. As you go into the phase of "Snake catches its prey" you are expanding the spleen area. As you go to the right side, you are squeezing out the large intestines. In addition, the added spiraling motion at the end of the movement will really open the spine.

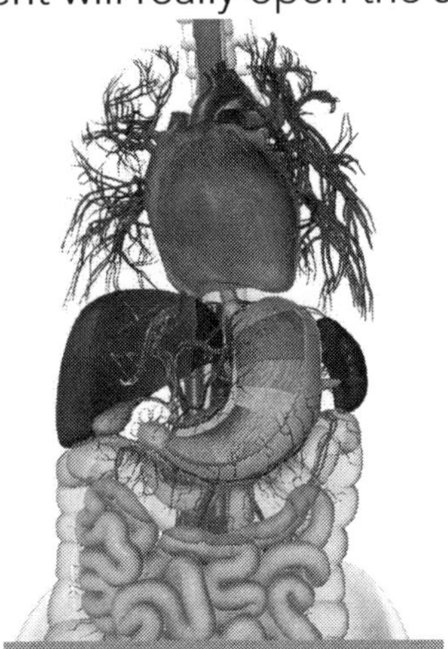
Lower Digestive System

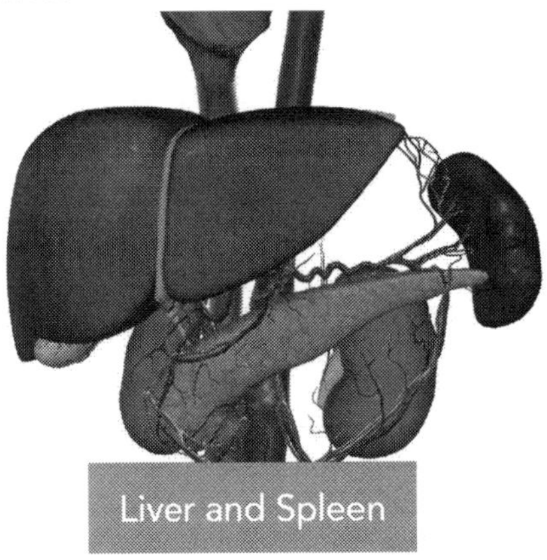
Liver and Spleen

## Effects on the Fascia

The fascia that the Snake works on also activates the Lateral Lines. By pushing the foot really firmly into the ground as you extend the body, you will tap into the Deep Front Line. Pushing the feet into the ground in Qigong is often called "rooting or "grounding". This Qigong feels like it goes deep into the body because it does go deep into the tissues when done correctly.

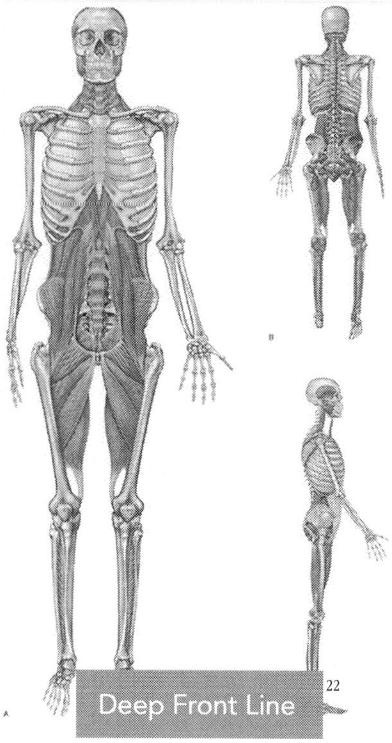

Deep Front Line[22]

There is an interplay between the Deep Front Line and the Lateral Line here as they create stability between the outside and the inside of the leg. You can really feel this again with the extension of the back leg and pushing the foot firmly into the ground. Feel the extension all the way into the hands. The twist at the end of the movement also activates the Spiral Line.

Additionally, as you pull the back arm back, it opens the Superficial Front Arm Line.

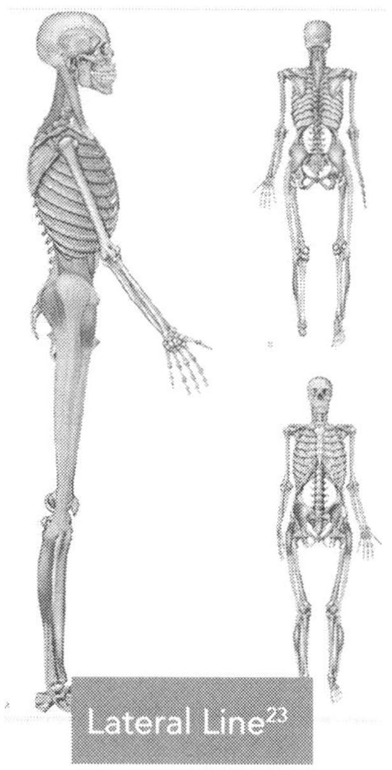

Lateral Line[23]

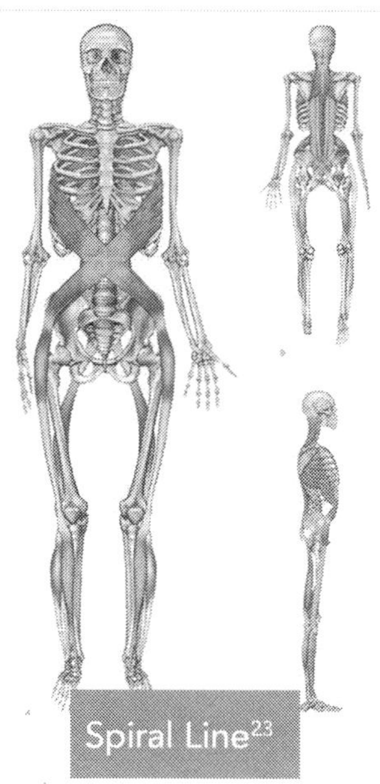

Spiral Line[23]

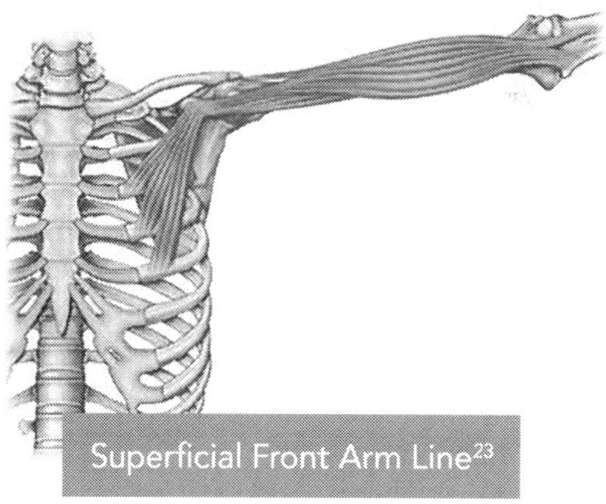

Superficial Front Arm Line[23]

[23] Reprinted from Anatomy Trains: Myofascial Meridians for Manual and Movement Therapists, 3E, Thomas Meyers, 2014, with permission from Elsevier

## Effects on the Meridians

The Snake activates the Spleen and Stomach Meridian

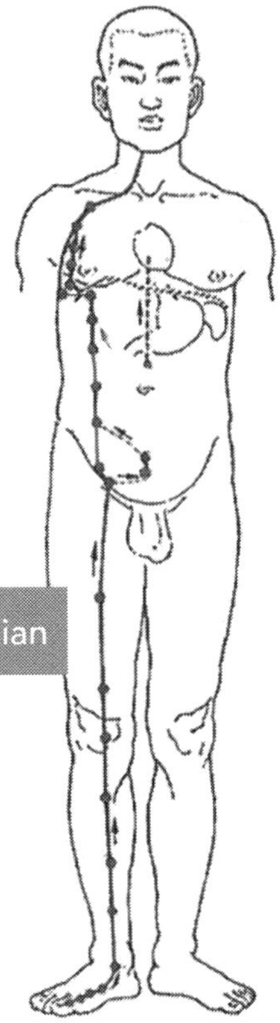


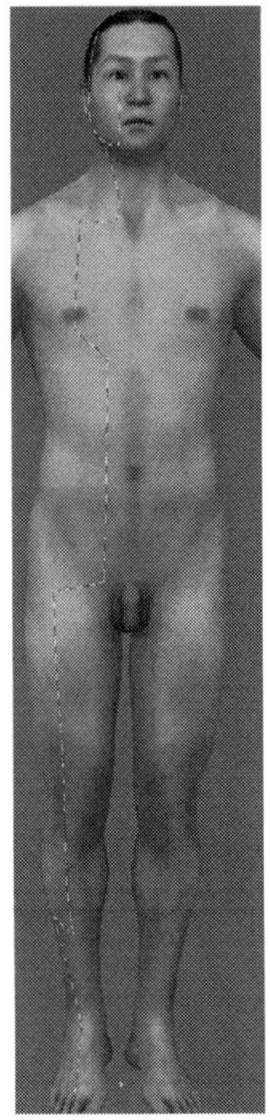

# About the Meridians

## The Spleen Meridian - For Self Esteem and Open Mindedness

### Function & Qualities

This meridian is a yin meridian and is paired with the stomach yang meridian.

**Element:** earth, with strong nurturing qualities

**Physical Imbalances:** digestive and stomach problems

**Emotional Imbalances:** worry, poor concentration, forgetful-ness, cloudy thought process, addiction, attachment, obsession, gluttony, jealousy, self-pity, strong concern about opinions of others, stubbornness, low self-esteem, poor self-image

**When Balanced:** fairness, openness, deep thinking and reminiscence, self esteem

**Peak Hours:** 9-11am

### Route

The spleen meridian starts at the tip of the big toe. From there it runs along the medial aspect of the foot at the junction where the skin tone changes color. It continues up the inner leg, up across the groin and the stomach, and through the diaphragm. It connects with the stomach and heart meridian.

## The Stomach Meridian – Assimilator of Physical and Emotional Nourishment

### Function & Qualities

The stomach meridian is a yang meridian and is paired with the spleen yin meridian.
It functions with the spleen meridian in the assimilation of Qi from food through digestion and absorption.

**Element:** earth, with strong nurturing qualities

**Physical Imbalances:** digestive and stomach problems - abdominal pain, distension, edema, vomiting, sore throat, facial paralysis, upper gum toothache, nose bleeding

**Emotional Imbalances:** anxiety, worry, skepticism, poor confidence, feelings of suspicion or mistrust

**When Balanced:** fairness, openness and caring

**Peak Hours:** 7-9am

### Route

The stomach meridian starts between the lower eyelid and the eye socket, and runs down the face, looping up to the forehead. It then backtracks down across the shoulder, down the ribs, along the stomach, and then down the leg ending on the outside edge of the second toe.

五元氣功

# THE CRANE

## Fire Element - Heart

*"The heart is the essence, the overlord of all internal organs of the six fu and five zhang. It is the abode of the spirit, and must be strong against outside evil or disease. If the outside evil influence has penetrated the heart, the heart will suffer such damage that the spirit will leave, and the human organism will die.[24]"*

The Crane is an animal of pure grace and beauty. In Chinese mythology, the crane represents longevity and peace. As the crane flies above the world, it is also considered a symbol of purity and cleanliness. There is a toast for birthdays in China, Japan and Korea that goes: "May your life be as long and as happy as that of a crane." It is also a symbol of high office, leadership, and nobility. Images of cranes were embroidered onto the robes of first ranking officials. Motifs of cranes in Chinese art are common, and while some are purely referring to the physical animal, some of those images have powerful symbolic meaning, including the representation of Taoist immortals (Xian), who were said to have the ability to transform into cranes.

Cranes live very long lives; the average lifespan is 20 to 30 years. They are highly social, and large flocks of cranes can be comprised of tens of thousands of birds. Cranes often stay with their mates their whole life span. Cranes dance for each other, bowing, bobbing their heads and spreading their wings. They may take grass or stones in their beaks and throw them in the air. Cranes seem to dance and jump for pure love and joy! Migrating cranes fly in a V-formation so that birds following the leader save energy. The birds can cruise at speeds of up to 45mph and glide over long distances, and the Siberian Crane may fly up to 10,000 miles in a year. The common crane is one of the highest-flying birds, flying over 33,000 feet over the Himalayas. Cranes, like tigers, are endangered. Out of the 15 types of crane, seven species are considered vulnerable to extinction.

In 5 Elements Theory, the Crane is associated with the element of fire, and with the heart. The heart is the color red.

The physical form is one of the easier ones to learn. As you practice, imagine this beautiful animal as it stands on one leg, stretches its wings, puffs out its chest and lands gracefully in a fluid motion.

[24] Optimal Healing, Patricia Tsang M.D, 2008

## Instructions

From the standing Qigong posture, again, open in the same way as the other movements. Choose a single point to stare at in front of you. This will focus your spirit. After the opening, allow both hands to open out towards the sides until they are parallel with the ground. From here, lift the left knee above the waist and extend the leg straight out with the toe pointed forward.

Balance on the right leg as the left leg circles out, around, and back. Point the fingers up towards the sky and open the arms backwards pushing your chest out towards the point you are staring at. Lean forward to lift the left leg as high as possible while keeping the head up and the arms level. This is the full extent of the motion. Hold this posture with a full breath for three to nine seconds.

From here, slowly drop the leg and return to the standing position before bringing the arms back down to the sides. To do the motion on the other side, simply raise the arms out to the sides again; it is not necessary to repeat the opening movements.

Completing the movements once on both sides makes one full round; three rounds make a set. Once done, repeat the closing movements three times before bringing the left foot in next to the right and letting the hands rest along the sides.

## Check Points

**Stance:**

- Front foot planted firmly in the ground
- Back foot behind you and feeling as if you are trying to touch your toes to your head
- Lower leg straight, or a micro-bend in the knee is fine

**Upper Body:**

- Fingers stretching straight up to the sky
- Opening the chest to the max to bring the heart out
- Back arched to the max

## Anatomical and Physiological Benefits

By really opening the chest, you allow your lungs and rib cage to move out of the way to open the heart area, bringing it forward. You open the chest during the inhalation phase to get a deeper inhalation. The arching compresses the kidneys, too.

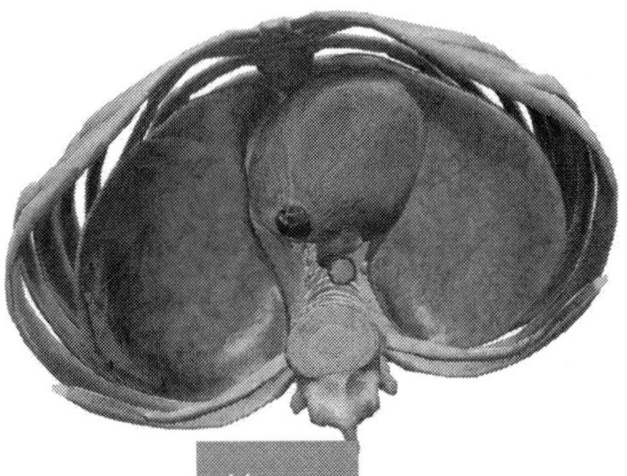

Heart

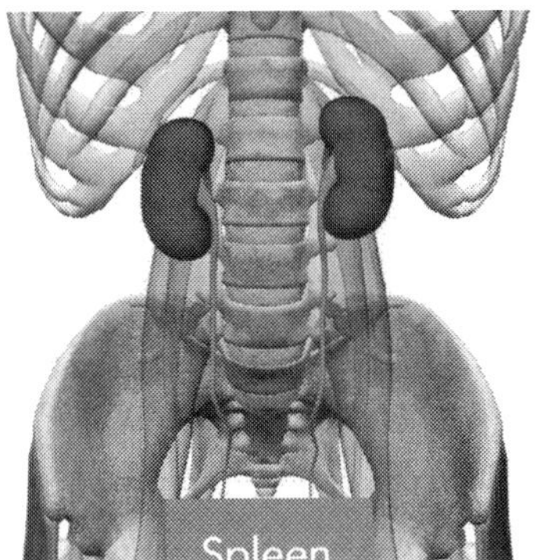

Spleen

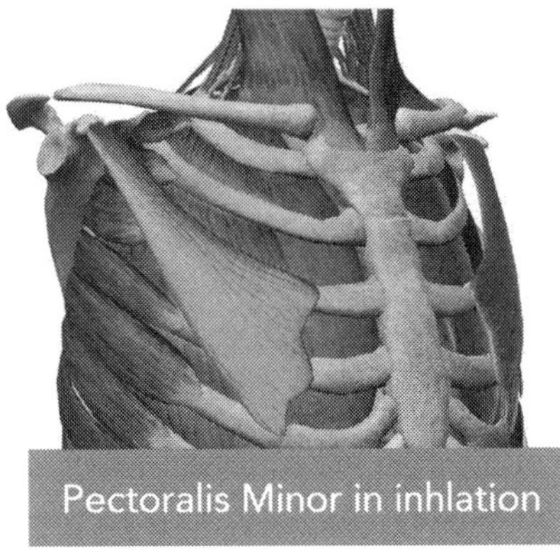

Pectoralis Minor in inhlation

It is said in Traditional Chinese Medicine that a patient with diseases of the heart may suffer from pain inside the chest, along and under the rib cage, and in the upper back as well as pain in the arms. The Crane addresses this, so it is important to correctly arch the back and open up the rib cage in coordination with the opening of the arms while practicing the form. Practitioners with more severe symptoms should practice a more static version of this and do so very gently.

## Effects on the Fascia

The Crane activates and opens the Superficial Front Arm Lines while using the Superficial Back Arm Lines to contract and pull on the Superficial Front Arm Lines.

By pulling up the back leg and arching the body, we contract the Superficial Back Line while stretching the Superficial Front Line.

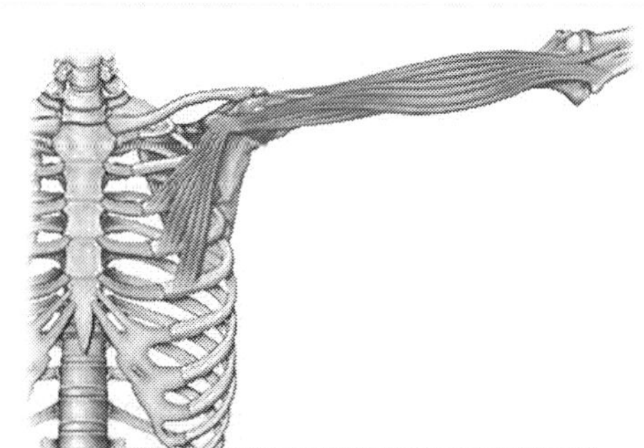

Superficial Front Arm Line[25]

## Effects on the Meridians

Spread out your arms and pull backwards, stretching the fingers, paying attention to the pinky finger in particular. Gently pronate the arms inwards to feel the meridian more deeply. Extend the wrist, raising the back of the hand to activate the acupuncture points underneath the wrist.

[25] Reprinted from Anatomy Trains: Myofascial Meridians for Manual and Movement Therapists, 3E, Thomas Meyers, 2014, with permission from Elsevier

# About the Meridians

## The Heart Meridian – House of the Spirit

### Function & Qualities

The heart meridian is a yin meridian and is paired with the small intestine meridian. It reveals itself through the brightness in the eyes, governs Fire and Heat, rules the blood and its vessels and directs circulation - it is the House of the Spirit. It also rules the tongue, throat, sweat, facial complexion, adrenals, thyroid, prostate and pituitary gland.

**Element:** Belonging to the Fire element, the Heart Meridian is associated with warmth, enthusiasm. Just as the summer season, associated with the Fire element, brings blossoming and maturing - the flowering of all the seeds planted in the spring - love is the blossoming of the human being. It is indeed who we are in full "bloom". Nowhere is such love felt more deeply than in the Heart.

**Physical Imbalances:** shortness of breath, cold feeling in the chest and limbs, palpitations, cold sweat, inability to speak, memory failure and restless sleep.

**Emotional Imbalances:** The heart is the ruler of all emotions. Signs of imbalance include sadness, absence of laughter, depression, fear, anxiety, hysteria, erratic behavior, alternating joy and melancholy, dullness, yearning for love, jealousy and sorrow.

**When balanced:** tranquility, gentleness, emotional balance, spirit, love, integrity, optimism, emotional and spiritual growth, zest for life, control of thoughts and senses, conscience and wisdom.

**Peak Hours:** 11am-1pm

### Route

It originates from the heart, emerges and spreads over the heart system, passes through the diaphragm to connect with the small intestine. The exterior (surface) running part runs to the lung, then turns downward along the arm. It ends in the inner tip of the little finger. In addition, it opens into the tongue and controls speech.

# The Small Intestine Meridian - Sorting of the Pure and Impure

## Function & Qualities

The small intestine meridian is a yang meridian and is paired with the heart yin meridian. It receives and transforms food by separating the Pure from the Impure, with the Pure becoming bodily fluids and the Impure becoming urine - this function also operates on emotional, mental and spiritual levels.

This meridian is responsible for digestion, water absorption, nutrient absorption and bowel functions.

**Element:** Fire

**Physical Imbalances:** Signs include bluish lips with white border, emaciation, profuse sweating, swellings of nodules, hemicrania, tinnitus, pain around the ear, and pain depressing the abdomen.

**Emotional Imbalances:** a feeling of mental deficiency due to inability to assimilate ideas, and insecurity. Forgetfulness, indecision, unclear thought process. Restlessness and difficulty in expressing emotions.

**When Balanced:** Healthy expressions are love, joy, warmth, vitality, excitement, memory, ability in making decisions, clarity of thought.

**Peak Hours:** 1-3pm

## Route

The Small Intestine Meridian starts from the tip of the little finger and crosses the wrist. It runs upwards along the posterior side of the forearm until it reaches the back of the shoulder, where it ends at the uppermost part of the back (the bottom of the neck). From this position, it travels externally across the neck and cheek until it reaches the outer corner of the eye and then ends in the ear.

五元氣功

# CLOSING

> *"It doesn't matter what you are doing now - when you are finished with it, you must let your heart/mind rest, even if it is just three or five minutes. If you sit in stillness for 15 minutes, you can cast everything away! In this way, you can slowly work to restore your original pure and clean heart. And this is something that cannot be bought by gold or money."*
>
> *Taoist Hermit Guo Gao Yi*

All Qigong exercise should include a closing sequence, which settles the body's energy back to the Dan Tian, calms the mind, and relaxes the body. We do this through Zhan Zhuang practice.

Bring the palms to the sides and face the palms up while positioning the feet at shoulder width apart. Inhale and at the same time bring the hands up, arching towards the center-line of your body. Once your hands reach the top of your head, face the palms downwards.

Exhale and press the Qi down your centerline with your fingertips facing each other. Passing through your Shang Dan Tian (Third Eye), then through your Zhong Dan Tian (heart), pressing all the way down to the Xia Dan Tian (Lower Dan Tian).

Once you reach this point, slowly relax your hands at your sides while keeping your fingers spread, without your hands touching the legs. Begin the deep Four Gate Breathing, inhaling into the Dan Tian and exhaling into the centers of the feet and palms. Do at least eight to 64 breaths depending on how you feel.

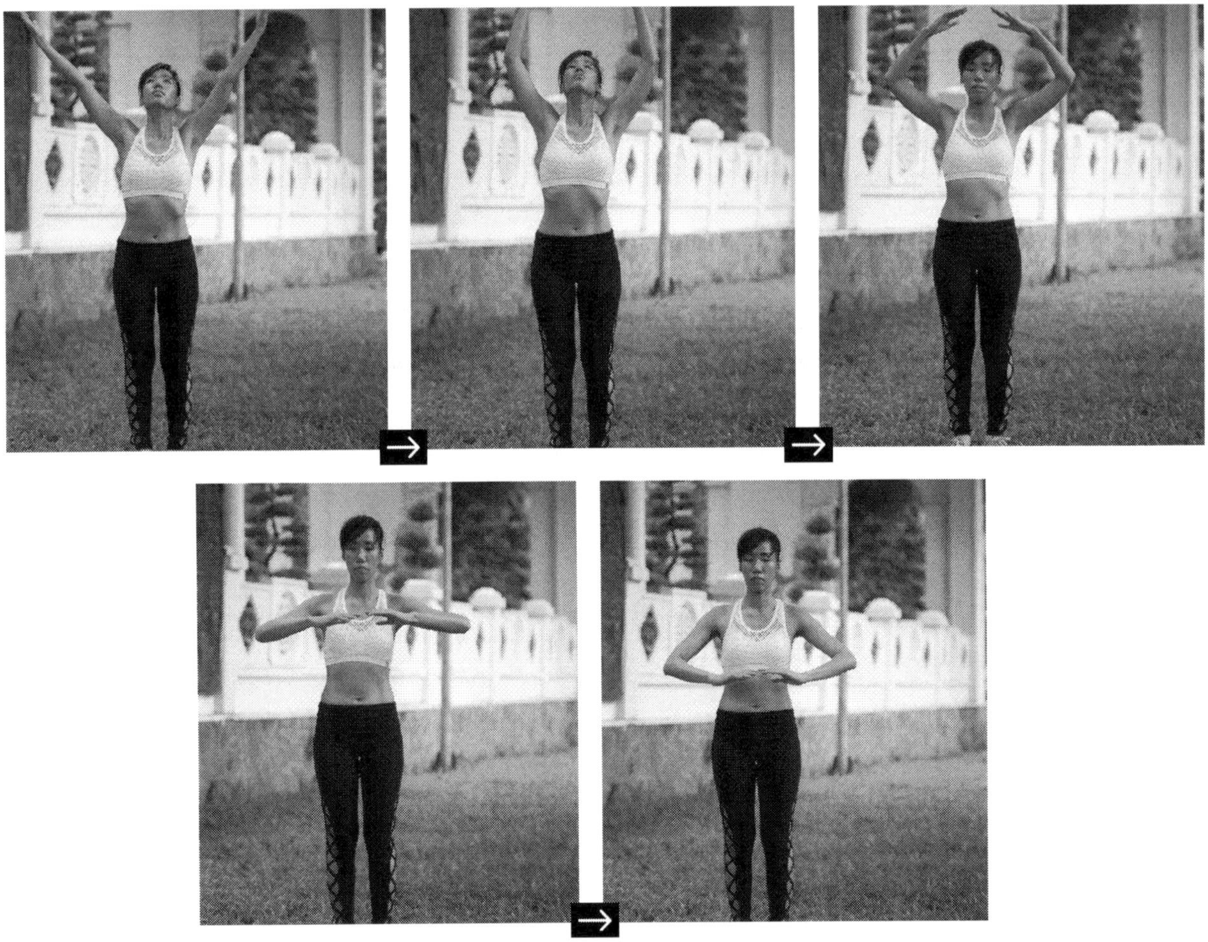

Upon completion of this, you have the option to continue with these Zhan Zhuang exercises or you can begin a final closing to your exercise.

## Final Closing

Once you complete these breaths, bring the palms over the Lower Dan Tian (left hand on the Dan Tian with right hand on top for males; the opposite for females). Breathe slow, deep breaths into the lower Dan Tian, feeling the Qi accumulating, gathering and condensing there. Slow down the breath and make it soft, long and thin like a thin silk thread.

Hold the thumb over the large intestine acupuncture point, which is the squishy part of the hand between the thumb and index finger. Place the thumb of the outside hand on the center of the palm of the inside hand. This is the Lao Gong point (pericardium point).

By activating these two acupuncture points, you help the Qi to sink, which is what we want at the end of our practice. It is important after finishing all the Qigong exercises, to do some deep breathing Qigong. Sports science has proven that deeper breathing after exercise is not only necessary for replenishment of oxygen, but also for elimination of carbonic acid.

Whenever we open or close at the beginning and end of Qigong, we focus on the Dan Tian to generate source Qi, harmonize the blood vessels and strengthen the spleen and stomach.

五元氣功

# ZHAN ZHUANG

> "Standing Qigong is the best posture for therapeutic breathing exercises, for it permits complete circulation of blood to all parts of the body and encourages free flow through the meridians. Standing also provides the best conduit between heaven and earth."
>
> *Daniel Reid*

Zhan Zhuang has many benefits and a multitude of purposes. Zhan Zhuang is one method we use to stop and check in with our body, to tune in to what is happening and observe the changes occurring after each Qigong exercise and also upon completion. This helps create a habit of checking in with yourself and becoming keenly aware of your body and the internal body. When you become accustomed to periodically checking in with how your body is feeling and performing, from when you wake up until the time you go to sleep, you can evaluate and treat small problems before they become big ones.

## Melting into Nothingness in Zhan Zhuang Qigong

This is a Taoist exercise of letting go of the physical body and melting into the energy of the universe. The Taoists believe this exercise calms the spirit, reduces wrinkles by relaxing the skin, completely relax the organs, and on a spiritual level brings you to new heights and understanding of the universe we live in. This exercise will help you sense and guide Qi on a more profound level.

## Instructions:

Assume the common Zhan Zhuang stance of legs at shoulder-width apart. Touch your tongue to the roof of your mouth. Then begin to gently and softly screw your legs into the earth to root and to open the sacrum, allowing it to drop naturally to the earth. Many people, even teachers, make the mistake of "tucking in the tailbone". This is an unnatural posture for the body as we have a natural curvature to the spine. Over time, if you repeatedly "tuck in the tailbone" you will distort the natural curvature and possibly create difficult spinal problems to overcome. I have even heard of a man whose teacher told him for many years to tuck in his tailbone until he eventually had to have corrective surgery to regain the curvature in his spine. I can therefore not overemphasize the importance of opening the hips so that the sacrum can naturally drop to the earth. This creates grounding and further rooting as you feel your perineum's natural pull towards the earth. Dropping the sacrum also stretches the lumbodorsal fascia.

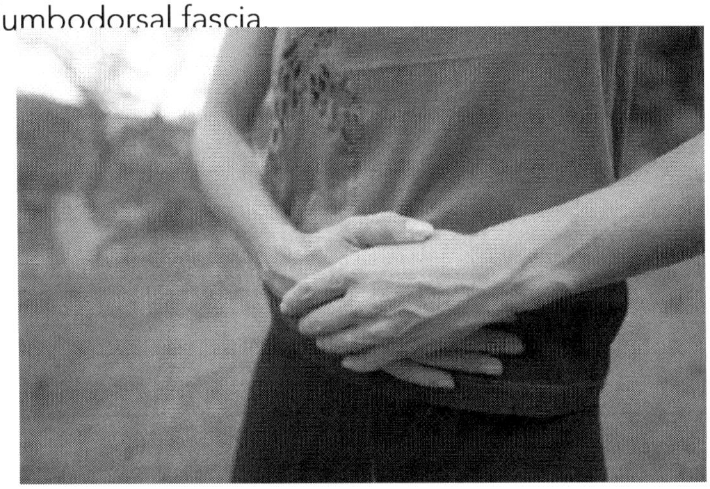

Now we want to build a proper structure so that the body holds itself up effortlessly. Gently spread out the toes and grab the ground with the toes using about 10% tension. This adds an even further root to the earth and also pulls up the Yong Quan point, which is the center of the foot, so the "bubbling spring" of Qi can start at the feet.

*Feel the knees over the ankles.*
*Feel the hips over the knees.*
*Feel the vertebrae over the hips, suspended over each other.*
*Feel the head resting on top of the spine, delicately balancing.*
*Feel a string from heaven holding up the head from the Crown Point.*
*Feel the sacrum being pulled towards the earth.*

This allows the spine to elongate naturally. The hands can be resting over the Dan Tian with the outside hand's thumb touching the Lao Gong point of the inside hand (the center of the palm), while the inside hand's thumb is touching the large intestine point (the squishy point between the thumb and the index finger). Think of this as if connecting a battery where the positive and negative meet. This will help generate an electrical charge.

Now that your structure is created and the palms are over the Dan Tian, begin to relax the body from the top down. When relaxing, it is best to sink your energy and to do this we start from the head to the feet. This is Yin as opposed to Yang, where when we raise energy we move it up.

While breathing deeply through the nose, inhale warm energy into the crown of your head. Fill that space with warm energy and imagine yourself like ice, where your skin and muscles are melting and the crown relaxing. Next, move down to the eyes, face, and jaw. Breathe in deeply into that area as if filling it with warm Qi and exhale through the nose, relaxing the forehead, eyes, eye sockets, cheeks, jaw, and even the back of the head as you relax the jaw. Then, down to the neck and throat, feel the energy melting and sinking down to the shoulders and arms all the way out into the hands and fingers, just like a wave of relaxation moving down your chest and upper back. Moving down to your solar plexus and mid-back, allow those areas to melt. Work your way down to your stomach, kidneys, and lower back. As you move towards your hips, relax your genitals, buttocks, and hips and feel them open. Melt the energy down your thighs, calves and finally down to the feet. Let go of your physical body. Keep breathing deeply, bring your mind to the navel and go deep inside the mysterious black hole.

You can focus on any area for as long as you need. Take as many breaths as you need until that area starts to relax.

Intermediate and advanced students might have some variations. There are three things to take into account during the Zhan Zhuang practice: posture, breath, and focusing the spirit.

The posture should be tall and relaxed. The feet should be parallel and placed shoulder-width apart with the weight evenly distributed; keep the knees soft but do not allow them to buckle inwards. Release the tension of the face, head, neck, shoulders, back, rear, thighs, and feet and allow the earth to completely support the body. You can use the visualization of ice melting to aid you in relaxing the body. This is also a visualization the Taoists use to dissolve the physical body.

The breath should be full and comfortable. Try to keep the breath slow, soft and even, at a rate of four to six breaths per minute. The external flow of breath is a reflection of the internal flow of energy; by regulating the breath, one can regulate the heart rate and Qi flow of the body, inducing relaxation and ease.

The intention should be focused but gentle. Allow the eyes to lightly gaze on the floor three to six feet ahead or keep the eyes closed. Keep the attention on the breath and concentrate it deep into the navel. Try to still the mind. Avoid distracting thoughts that take the mind off of the present moment of practice.

In Zhan Zhuang, total relaxation of the body involves softening the muscles and tendons. After circulating the Qi deep inside the body and after thorough dynamic movement of compression, expansion, twisting and rotation, thus squeezing out the organs and meridians, you will be able to relax into Zhan Zhuang much more deeply. Correcting the alignment while allowing the tendons to relax is important. The back should not be tense at all when standing.

Do seated practice after becoming completely relaxed.

## Skin Breathing

An alternative to focusing on the lower Dan Tian is to feel as if each breath you take is drawn through the pores of your skin, bringing the energy into the lower Dan Tian and as you exhale you breathe back out of your pores. Thus, you are exchanging energy with the universe. This is believed to be good for the skin and, after some practice, you may actually feel that your skin is breathing. This is also a great way to allow the feeling and perception of the physical body to "melt" into the universe.

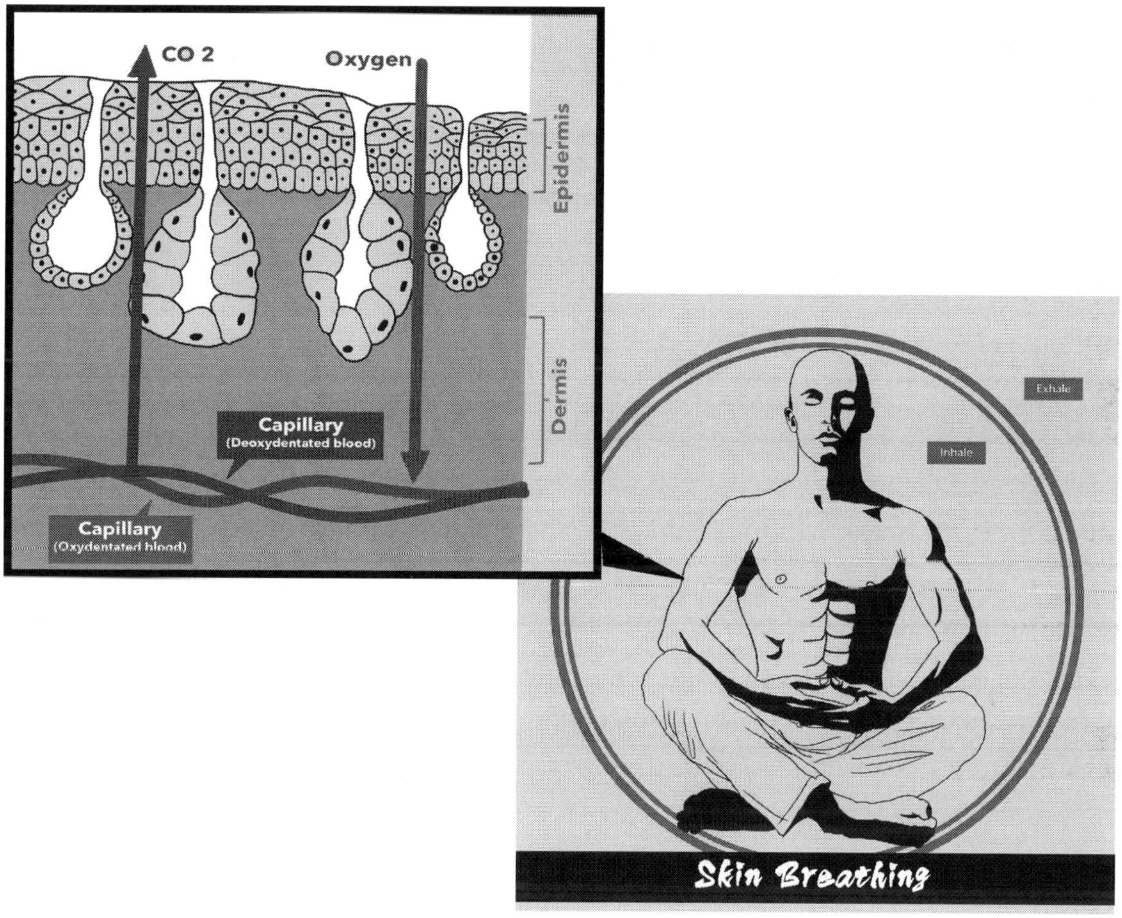

五元氣功

# Conclusion

## Healing Yourself with Qigong

White Tiger Qigong™ is used for deep healing of all kinds, including emotional trauma, physical injuries, difficult to treat diseases, cancer and more. It is often times used in conjunction with Traditional Chinese Medicine herbal concoctions, acupuncture, massage, outgoing Qi therapies, group energy field healing and more. We encourage our students to take responsibility for their own health situation through the practice of Qigong and other longevity exercises, and most importantly through changing their own thoughts and behaviors. It should be repeated; being cured of disease does not give one the license to return to previous habits, as these things were what often what caused the disease or ailment in the first place. One was cured of disease for a purpose, in order to create a new self and a new life. If one returned to former lifestyle habits and ways of thought, the disease and symptoms would be likely to return. The White Tiger Qigong™ School is not a hospital, but a place where people come to discover how to regulate their bodies and spirit.

White Tiger Qigong™ should ideally serve as a catalyst for a kind of sacred metamorphosis in which, with a new healthy body, so too emerges a new personality with nascent enlightened forms of perception and behavior. Daoist Medical Qigong also serves as a means for the practitioner to help teach others how to relieve their own suffering while spiritually elevating themselves, which is one of many paths that can lead to a higher understanding of the Dao. The ultimate goal of White Tiger Qigong™ is to help elevate each other from suffering while promoting healing, transformation and the realization of your ultimate potential.

## The Theory and the Practice

Progressing from the basics to the advanced level is the law to follow in Qigong. Higher levels of Qigong will only be reached step-by-step with persistent, dedicated practice. In our modern society, we are always looking for shortcuts, "hacks" or ways to get ahead quicker than others. I sometimes have to remind my students that Qigong is not a competition (although they do have those, too). You cannot reach a master level in one day. What you can do is master one form at a time until you have mastered that level. The general practical skills of Qigong are not hard to learn. Thus, one can become proficient in a single form of Qigong in a relatively short period of time. I have seen some master the movements of a form in a month while others struggle for a year. This depends on the individual's existing body awareness, coordination and focus. The theory can be taught in a day, but to truly integrate it takes time, with true body and spirit awareness. This can only come with lots of practice; there are no shortcuts. When you can stay in one state during your exercise from beginning to end, you have mastered the form. This takes concentration and practice.

Qigong practice is a process of accumulation. I remember when I was 19 years old, I was doing an intense 45 minutes of Zhan Zhuang two times per day over six months. I stopped for only two weeks and it took me a month to get back the level of Qi I lost during those two weeks. If you are just looking for the benefits of Qigong, many practitioners can get positive effects in just several sessions while others may take more time.

After you have read all the theory and absorbed it, let go of it and focus on your practice. Interestingly enough, I have heard that the practitioners who have the most profound effects from Qigong as a form of therapy are farmers because they are simple; they don't care to know about the theory so much and their mind is open. My master said to spend less time talking and more time practicing. He meant don't spend too much time on theory or else you will lose the essence of the practice. Now that you have finished this book, put it down and go practice!

# To Your Health *and* Longevity!

Tevia Feng
Founder of White Tiger Qigong™
WhiteTigerQigong.com

# Special Offer *for* Readers

Thank you for purchasing a White Tiger Qigong™ educational product. This book has an accompanying online course which you can find at www.whitetigerqigong.com. This provides in depth details of every animal, an entire course on fascia and its relationship to this Qigong by renowned anatomy expert Chris Kummer, as well as the 5 Elements of Ancient Chinese Medicine and its relationship to the 5 Animal Qigong.

Tevia Feng is the Master Instructor and Founder of White Tiger Qigong™. He began martial arts, Qigong and meditation training at the age of 7. He has personally taught thousands of students from around the world. He has worked with cancer sufferers, professional athletes, ballet dancers, yogis, martial artists, CEO's and the common folk. He has lived and traveled throughout China, studying various martial art forms - including rare forms of Qigong - with various masters, hermits and Taoist masters at multiple Taoist monasteries and temples.

Find out more about this knowledgeable author on

https://whitetigerqigong.com/about-us/tevia-feng/

Now that you have read the 8 Element Qigong book, you may be interested in reading more about the subject on https://whitetigerqigong.com/ or download our Free eBook: Secrets of the Centenarians at https://whitetigerqigong.com/secrets-of-centenarians-ebook/

Get a ***15% discount*** on our Dynamic 5 Animal Flow Qigong online course on any one of our courses: please use this code: onlinecoursedisc15

We would love to interact with you, and invite you to connect with our online community on:

**facebook.com/groups/853125531364585/**

## Follow us on Social Media

facebook.com/whitetigerqigong

plus.google.com/+Whitetigerqigong/

instagram.com/whitetigerqigong

twitter.com/teviafeng

youtube.com/ user/tigerqigong

id.pinterest.com/qigongarts/

You are also more than welcome to attend any, or all, of our events; follow what we're doing and when on https://whitetigerqigong.com/events/

Please see our website for information on other books in this range.

30073839R00087

Printed in Great
Britain
by Amazon